In His Image

Written by
Michael E. Lanphere

Holly Brook Baptist Church
3219 S. FM 2869
Hawkins, TX 75765-4732

Copyright © 2010 by Michael E. Lanphere

In His Image
by Michael E. Lanphere

Printed in the United States of America

ISBN 9781615798070

All rights reserved solely by the author. The author guarantees all contents are original and do not infringe upon the legal rights of any other person or work. No part of this book may be reproduced in any form without the permission of the author. The views expressed in this book are not necessarily those of the publisher.

www.xulonpress.com

714·351·2301
? 903·613·2275

P 163

Holly Brook Baptist Church
3219 S. FM 2869
Hawkins, TX 75765-4732

Table of Contents

Acknowledgements vii
Preface ix
Foreword xi
A Word about Personality Assessment Questionnaires xv

Chapter 1
    Viewpoints and Theories 23

Chapter 2
    Overview of the Biblical Man 33

Chapter 3
    Overview of the Myers-Briggs Type Indicator 40

Chapter 4
    Comparing the Two Attitudes of Introversion and
        Extraversion 52

Chapter 5
    Comparing the Two Perceiving Functions:
        Sensing and Intuition 71

Chapter 6
    Issues that Impact the Two Judging Functions:
        Thinking and Feeling 90

Chapter 7
  Comparing the Two Judging Functions:
    Thinking and Feeling 98

Chapter 8
  Comparing the Two Attitudes of Judging
    and Perceiving 122

Chapter 9
  Introduction to Temperament 140

Chapter 10
  The SP – Artisan 148

Chapter 11
  The SJ – Guardian 163

Chapter 12
  The NT – Rational 179

Chapter 13
  The NF – Idealist 195

Chapter 14
  Conclusion 211

Appendix A
  Four Communication Styles 213

Acknowledgements

I want to thank some very special people who helped me with the writing of this book. Mike & JoAnn Clark who provided an isolated, quite and comfortable place to write a good portion of the book and also JoAnn's insights to the characteristics of the INTJ. Also Raisa Wilfong who taught me so much about the ENFP as we worked together in ministry for so many years. Daivd and Kim deCarvalho who are missionaries with Youth With A Mission and Directors of the Introduction To Biblical Counseling School. They gave Linda and I our start with YWAM and continue to support us and invite us back to teach at YWAM Bases around the world. Most of all I would like to thank my wife Linda. Without her this book and my knowledge of the contents of this book would not exist. We have spent many hours together not just teaching but going through workshops, certification processes, and talking about the subject of Personality and Temperament differences, our own and others. I thank God for His Word that will bring needed balance to the way we use the wonderful tools He has given each us in order to function in this world.

Preface

My wife and I have been teaching "In His Image", a relationship development seminar to pre-martial's, married couples and singles since 1980. Using the Myers Briggs™ and the Keirsey Temperament™ theories, combined with Biblical principles for relationships we have seen people come to a new understanding of their own and others unique and predictable God given characteristics. As a result people have been awakened to inborn abilities that had previously been dormant and have improved their understanding of themselves and others.

In 1987 we had our first experience with the University of Nations, the educational arm of Youth With a Mission. We were invited to teach "In His Image" at Maka Pala a YWAM base on the big Island of Hawaii. Since that time we have conducted numerous seminars for YWAM, primarily in their "Introduction to Biblical Counseling" school and secondarily in their Crossroads school. Since that first experience at Maka Pala, we have presented this material at The University of Nations in Kona, Hawaii, remote bases at Velar, Lausanne, and Chatel, Switzerland, Santiago, Chile and Salem Oregon. As of this writing we have been traveling to YWAM bases for 23 years, challenging students to become all that God has created them to be. In each experience we have been enriched by seeing God's hand at work in revealing to individuals these truths; They are His creation, *"fearfully and wonderfully made"* with a divine purpose for their lives and they are *"ministers of reconcilia-*

tion" called to be an extension of God's healing hand to individuals struggling in life.

The primary goal of this book is to equip people with tools that will help them minister effectively to others. The Gospel is imparted most effectively through the development of an honest and caring relationship with others. This can only be achieved when we learn to recognize, respect, and understand the differences in people and their unique way of approaching life. Notice I didn't say their "philosophy of life" – that's too subjective and too often void of the truth that sets men free. I'm speaking of those personality characteristics that are inborn and that may be inherently different from our own particular characteristics. Most people see life from their perspective alone, and consequently they believe their perception is the "right" perception. This approach can be very limiting. This book hopes to challenge that mindset while helping people gain greater understanding of those who approach life from a different viewpoint.My wife Linda and I use the Myers-Briggs Personality Theory as an integral part of our seminars. A close study of this theory reveals that there are unique concepts each person will relate to and find helpful in developing deeper and more meaningful relationships in his or her life. It's my belief that for the most part, our time on this earth is to be spent impacting people for the sake of the kingdom of God. Any tool that will help us accomplish this goal is a tool worthy of use.The MBTI™ has been a very effective tool for Linda and me, especially in our own marriage. We have also used it for years in premarital and marriage counseling, and it has consistently given people insight as to their personality differences as well as how to appreciate those differences. When we teach relationship principles from God's Word coupled with personality dynamics, people begin to understand one another, sometimes for the first time, and the result is that marriages are healed and family relationships are restored. It is our prayer that those traveling with us on this journey will not only learn to appreciate the unique differences in others but will also discover the freedom to be who God created them to be.

Forward

Let me begin with a little bit of our personal history. Linda and I have been married since 1969 and we're still going strong. We have a great relationship and it just keeps getting better. I believe the reason I can say this is because we've learned that hard work pays off. We have put a lot of time into understanding one another, and it has been worth every minute of effort. We continue to make an effort to apply relationship principles that we learn from the Bible, but we are not foolish enough to believe that we've "arrived." There will always be more to learn about each other and those with whom we relate. The pressures and seasons of life, health problems, and loss constantly remind us that change happens, and when it does, suddenly we're viewing life from a new dimension.

However, I can't say that Linda and I related well to each other from day one. This brings me to why we have chosen to write this book. After about ten years of marriage, Linda (whom I love dearly) began to change quite drastically. She was no longer the effervescent, fun-loving, spontaneous woman I had met twelve years earlier when we began dating. She had gradually become more withdrawn, and in her desire to please me she had restricted her natural behavior in order to become what she thought I wanted her to be; in effect, she had given up much of whom God created her to be. I was largely responsible for this change in her personality, though I didn't realize it at the time. Without knowing it, I was working hard to get her and everyone else in our family to do things my way, because after all, I had everyone's best interest in mind and knew the "best way" to do things, to see things, to hear things, and so on. For some reason I thought everyone should be looking at life through the same lenses I used. Any behavior outside of how I would do things needed to be corrected, and it usually didn't take me long to make the corrections. In retrospect, I thank God for a friend who suggested I read a book titled *Please Understand Me*.[1] The following is an excerpt from the first chapter, which is titled "Different Drums and Different Drummers":

> If I do not want what you want, please try not to tell me that my want is wrong; or if I believe other than you, at least pause before you correct my view; or if my emotion is less than yours or more, given the same circumstances, try not to ask me to feel more strongly or weakly; or yet if I act, or fail to act, in the manner of your design for action, let me be. I do not, for the moment at least, ask you to understand me. That will come only when you are willing to give up changing me into a copy of you.

While reading that short paragraph I saw a perfect description of myself hidden within its words. I was the one expecting everyone to conform to my way. This realization, accompanied by the conviction of the Holy Spirit, was enough to drive me deep into the book, where I hoped to find out more about my behavior as well as really discover my wife and kids for the first time. This journey started in 1981.

I thought I was doing a good job of being a husband and father, and when it came to providing and protecting my family, taking care of all of their physical needs, I was. However, I was failing horribly when it came to understanding my wife and kids. I really had not taken the time to learn to apply the Golden Rule in our relationship:

> *Therefore, whatever you want others to do for you, do also the same for them—this is the Law and the Prophets (Matthew 7:12)* HCSB

---

[1] *Please Understand Me: Character and Temperament Types*, David Keirsey and Marilyn Bates, Prometheus Nemesis Book Company.

In His Image

The *"do also the same for them"* is the hard part. It is a challenge to understand the people we're in relationship with. In fact, the little word "do" is the key, but it presents the perplexing question: Do what? The answer is very simple: Do those things that will bless the other person. I'm an avid cyclist. I could take Linda on a date to watch the bicycle races and I would be thrilled to be there, but it wouldn't be the first thing on Linda's fun list. But because I learned to understand her interests, I have a good idea of what I should do to bless her. It would be something along the lines of going to a dinner theater or taking a trip to the San Diego Zoo, or going shopping with her at the mall or just taking a quick, spontaneous trip to get some frozen yogurt. Jesus didn't say it would be easy. In fact, by giving us the Golden Rule He provided us with insight into the character of our heavenly Father:

Every generous act and every perfect gift is from above, coming down from the Father of lights (James 1:17). HCSB

The idea here is to be the giver. The Bible says God knows what to give us even before we ask. (Matthew 6:32) NKJV

For after all these things the Gentiles seek. For your heavenly Father knows that you need all these things

How does He know? He knows each one of us individually; He knows our interests, our gifts, our calling and our purpose, as well as those personality quirks that, when combined with everything else, make each of us so unique. The "wish" part of the verse takes care of itself because the principle of sowing and reaping comes into play. It's absolutely amazing how Linda and I have really experienced the "oneness" of marriage ever since we began taking the time and making the effort to get to know and understand each other in such an intimate way. We're both blessed as we make an effort to offer our resources to one another physically, spiritually, and emotionally.

Gradually, as I stopped trying to get Linda to conform to my image of the perfect wife, I saw her once again blossoming into that woman I had first met, the one who was full of life. I realized I had been forcing her into a position of trying to live life on borrowed behavior. That will work for a while, but eventually it will come crashing down. God has created each of us uniquely, with a particular call and purpose for our life, and when I began to appreciate Linda for who she was (and is), and I even helped and encouraged her to make discoveries about herself, she began to bloom again, and she has become even more beautiful to me.

Why Should You Read On?

This is a book about you and people you relate with. Before you answer the questions on the assessment you must ask yourself some questions; *Do I want to know why I function in life as I do? Am I going to be "categorized", or will this experience show my individual uniqueness? Do I want to know my natural strengths and weaknesses? Do I want to know my core needs, those emotional needs that go beyond my physical needs? Do I want to know if I'm in the best fit vocation? Do I want to know about differences between me and my spouse, family members or friends?* The Assessment you're about to respond to will become a very revealing tool for you as you continue on in this book. But I must warn you, this is not a novel that you would read for entertainment. From this point on it will take an honest and open assessment of yourself as you continue. You will better understand the subsequent chapters if you have an idea of your own four letter Myers Briggs personality type. Therefore I am inserting a short questionnaire that will get you started.

A Word about Personality Assessment Questionnaires

There are many personality questionnaires available both online and in book form, and most of them are fairly accurate. If you do an Internet search using the keywords "Myers-Briggs," you'll find several resources that are free of charge and that include a personality questionnaire, and many of them will even score it for you.

Linda and I always tell our students that the questionnaire is just the starting point to understanding your personality type and thus who you are, whether you pay $75.00 for an assessment of your responses or you pay nothing. We have used elaborate questionnaires and very simple questionnaires, and the results have been very similar. They are about 70% to 80% accurate overall.

Providing answers for a questionnaire like this is a good starting point for learning about your personality type. But you'll make your greatest discoveries about yourself and lay a solid foundation as you go through the learning process in the following pages of this book.

As we examine the various traits and functions of personality in this book, please let this experience be one of personal revelation for you – look eagerly for "ah-ha" moments regarding your personality. It is typical during our weeklong seminars for 30% to 40% of the students to change one or more of the four letters by the end of the class as they gain clarity on their personality type.

When answering any questionnaire, think about what you really prefer and what you already like to do, not what you think is required of you or expected of you by someone else in the myriad of environments you've experienced. Doing so will only add to your confusion; thus, you never want to answer questions based on who you would like to be, but instead, always answer them truthfully about who you already are.

We have found the following questionnaire to work pretty well, it is also simple and quick. It will take you about ten minutes to finish. For best results answer the questions quickly, and try to remove environmental requirements on your life as you think about your answers. It's all about how you prefer to function in life.

Take a moment to determine your personality type:

Take a moment to determine your personality type:

This is a list of opposite statements. Circle the letter of the statement you relate to most. Do not circle both. The opposite letters are A or B, C or D, E or F, G or H.

1. **A** – I'm energized by being around people.
   B – I regain energy by being alone.

2. **C** – I perceive and give tangible information.
   D – I look for meanings and possibilities; I seek to understand how things relate to one another.

3. **E** – I follow principles when making decisions; logic is one of most important principles.
   F – I make decisions based on values, meaning, things that are important to others and to me.

4. **G** – I prefer to be organized and orderly.
   H – I prefer to experience and understand the world I live in.

In His Image

5. **A** – When I'm interacting with others, I tend to jump right in.
    B – I set and respect boundaries.

6. **C** – I see the real world, and I understand its limitations.
    D – I prefer my imagination and the feeling of having limitless potential.

7. **E** – I focus on content; I screen out emotions.
    F – I focus on personal considerations; emotions are a comfortable part of the process.

8. **G** – I'm good at making lists and outlining plans.
    H – I prefer flexibility. Plans can be too confining.

9. **A** – I will make the first move when meeting people for the first time.
    B – I will wait for someone else to make the first move and approach me.

10. **C** – I see sequentially and I grasp the details.
    D – I see conceptually, and I grasp the big picture.

11. **E** – I can confront strongly; but in doing so, sometimes I hurt others unintentionally.
    F – I can empathize with others, and I avoid confrontation.

12. **G** – I can be too focused and miss new information.
    H – I can be overwhelmed by too many opportunities.

13. **A** – I show the world who I am readily and easily.
    B – I have an important hidden side.

14. **C** – I see solutions to practical, concrete problems.
    D – I see solutions to complex or theoretical problems.

15. **E** – To me, fairness is very important in relationships.
    F – To me, appreciation is important in relationships.

In His Image

16. G – I see time in terms of a decision.
    H – I see time in terms of an opportunity.

17. A – I'm good at fast, spontaneous conversations.
    B – I weigh carefully what I say.

18. C – I'm specific and literal when speaking.
    D – I'm general and abstract when speaking.

19. E – I can survive without harmony.
    F – Unresolved conflict is very stressful to me.

20. G – Time pressure can force me to make premature decisions.
    H – So many opportunities make it hard for me to decide which one to choose.

21. A – I solidify and clarify my thoughts by talking them out with someone else.
    B – I solidify and clarify my thoughts by inward contemplation.

22. C – I focus on specifics to carry out the task.
    D – I like to develop new concepts.

23. E – I tend to be brief and concise in my communication.
    F – I am more sociable and friendly in my communication.

24. G – I believe I know the most expedient way to do things, and I don't mind telling others.
    H – I prefer to see new ways to do things; I'm interested in the process more than the result.

25. A – I have broad friendships with many different people.
    B – I have deep friendships with a very few people.

In His Image

26. **C** – I like people to say what they mean and mean what they say.
    D – I prefer hearing metaphors and parables.

27. **E** – Most often, my head rules my heart
    F – Most often, my heart rules my head.

28. **G** – I am usually early rather than late.
    H – I am usually late rather than early.

Count the letters you circled and place the totals under the corresponding Letter in the grid below. Circle the four letters on the bottom row that have a number higher than 3. That will be your Myers-Briggs Type.

LiLi = INFJ

A	B	C	D	E	F	G	H
3	4	5	3	3	4	4	3
7		5	2		6	5	2
E	I	S	N	T	F	J	P

DON = ESFJ

To get Your Temperament Type circle the one of the four combinations below that contain two of your MBTI Letters.

Lillie SJ

SP   SJ   NT   NF
5-5   2-6

SOME REASONS PEOPLE DISTORT THEIR ANSWERS

Extraversion Verses Introversion (E vs. I)

The western world has a tendency to reward extraverted behavior. Just watch the commercials on television to see evidence of this tendency. The Extravert is considered the "life of the party" or the one with the "great personality" – the ones who are "friendly" and "exciting." I'm not saying this is a negative thing regarding Extraverts, but it is obvious that the world looks at Extraverts differently than how Introverts are perceived. On the contrary, Introverts are typically described as being shy; as being the "wallflowers" at a social gathering; or they're even considered as unfriendly and boring. With this in mind there could be some negative images in the minds of true Introverts. Naturally, with this mentality so prevalent in our society today, some Introverts are secretly Extravert wannabes. When this is the case, they have a tendency to lean toward Extraversion when answering questionnaires. Be aware of this tendency and keep in mind that one trait is not better than another, they are simply different.

Sensing and INtuition (S vs. N; "I" is in use so we use "N" for Intuition.)

Over the years, we have found that because Sensors see things in black and white, no grey areas they will generally answer questions with a very clear distinction, confirming that they are Sensors. On the other hand, when Intuitives answer questions, it is much more difficult for them to find answers that suit their nature exactly, and some Intuitives even score as Sensors. The majority believe they could go either way in their responses and still be giving honest answers. Many times Intuitives begin the information–gathering process with their Senses and then shift to using their Intuition in order to see the possibilities or potential this new information brings with it. Most Sensors don't trust their Intuition and are perfectly content with gathering information through tangible means.

Thinking and Feeling (T vs. F)

It is estimated that 70% of the male population in the United States are Thinkers and 30% are Feelers. Correspondingly 70% of the female population are Feelers and 30% are Thinkers. With this being the case, there is pressure on men to behave and interact like Thinkers with their matter-of-fact and sometimes insensitive approach to life. That leaves 30% of males who don't quite fit the mold, as they tend to be relational and sensitive to people they're in relationship with. Because of this men who score somewhat close to Feeling should take a close look at the Feeling traits in the chapter relating to Thinking and Feeling. The same thing is true with the 30% of females who are Thinkers. People are expecting them to be very sensitive, understanding, and easy to approach, but in reality, they challenge decisions and are straightforward in their communication style. Many times it is surprising and even intimidating to men (and to other women as well) when Thinking women display their ability to get involved and "mix it up" verbally with others. I'm always concerned when people write about male/female differences and they leave out this important truth. So many men and women have been set free by understanding this crucial aspect of their personality and realizing they are okay, and their ability as a Feeler for the males and Thinker for the females is part of God's design for them. Many notable characters in the Bible fall into this minority: men who are Feelers and women who are Thinkers. And when it comes to answering personality questionnaires, Feeler men (F) and Thinker (T) women struggle a little more with corresponding questions than do those who fall into their genders majority.

Judgers and Perceivers (J vs. P)

When you're born into a production oriented country like the US or Japan, you're expected to operate like a Judger whether that's your preference or not. There is overwhelming environmental pressure to behave in certain ways. True Judgers fit right in with this type of culture. On the other hand, Perceivers like to take things as they come without all the planning, structure and time limits that Judgers love to impose on their environment, on others, and on themselves. Since many Perceivers have gotten themselves in trouble over the years whenever they've done what comes naturally to them, that is, live a much more laid back open ended lifestyle, they struggle with answering personality questionnaires as well.

Obviously, many other factors come into play when answering questionnaires. Any extenuating environmental pressure will impact the development of our personality and our perception of how we prefer to live.

The goal of this book is to help you discover your real strengths and to embrace them. Being who you are and not who someone else wants you to be will change not only the quality of your life but the way you live life. My prayer is that you will make the effort to finish this book and begin to put your newfound knowledge and understanding to work in all of your relationships. You'll be glad you did.

CHAPTER 1

VIEWPOINTS AND THEORIES

As previously stated, Linda and I teach on the subject of personality characteristics using adaptations of the Myers-Briggs Personality Type and the Keirsey-Bates Temperament theories. I use the word adaptations because of the integration of scriptural insight about behavioral characteristics that Linda and I bring to the table. Typically, secular psychology and biblical teaching go off in different directions at some point. In cases such as these, we choose to follow what the Bible has to say about human behavior. With that said, we don't throw the baby out with the bath water either. Although both Isabel Briggs-Myers and David Keirsey built their theories based on the ideas of those who came before them, the behavioral discoveries made by both are incredibly accurate, and in many ways, they prove to be self-evident concerning human personality and temperament. The Myers-Briggs theory defines and breaks down aspects of our personality into individual elements, such as whether we're an Extravert or an Introvert, and how we gather information and evaluate it. These elements are considered to be inborn and will remain with us all of our lives. David Keirsey, on the other hand, looks at temperament in its entirety, which includes certain inborn predispositions. In an example from his book *Please Understand Me II,* he explains, "There are two sides to personality, one of which is temperament and the other is character. Temperament is a configuration of inclinations, while character is a configuration of habits. Character is disposition; temperament is predisposition. Thus, for example, foxes are predisposed – born

– to raid hen houses, beavers to dam up streams, dolphins to affiliate in close knit schools, owls to hunt in the dark ... thus, temperament is the inborn form of human nature; character, the emergent form, which develops through the interaction of temperament and environment."[2] Neither right or wrong they are simply two different ways to look at human behavior, in fact they compliment one another in helping people get a clearer picture of their traits.

Keirsey's description of temperament and character as it relates to human behavior falls in line with many Jungian psychologists' approach to understanding human behavior. From my perspective, as a man of faith who believes in intelligent design and the impact of spiritual rebirth, these definitions fall short. It's a mixed bag. There are many truths in Keirsey's theory regarding human behavior, but there is another dimension that he never discusses, which has the ultimate impact on human behavior: the spiritual dimension; specifically, our spiritual condition before and after we come to know Christ.

I cannot study human behavior without including this third dimension. My perspective is this: Scripture is clear concerning each person's uniqueness, which includes having a God-designed purpose and call in life. This is evidenced in passages such as Psalm 139:13-16 that says:

> *For You formed my inward parts;*
> *You covered me in my mother's womb.*
> *I will praise You, for I am fearfully and wonderfully made;*
> *Marvelous are Your works,*
> *And that my soul knows very well.*
> *My frame was not hidden from You,*
> *When I was made in secret,*
> *And skillfully wrought in the lowest parts of the earth.*
> *Your eyes saw my substance, being yet unformed.*
> *And in Your book they all were written,*
> *The days fashioned for me,*
> *When as yet there were none of them. (NKJV)*

---

[2] Page 20, *Please Understand Me II: Temperament, Character, Intelligence*, David Keirsey, Prometheus Nemesis Book Company.

and Jeremiah 1:4-5:

> *Then the word of the LORD came to me, saying: "Before I formed you in the womb I knew you; Before you were born I sanctified you; I ordained you a prophet to the nations." (NKJV)*

These passages are quite clear and specific about the call and purpose of each human being. Furthermore, there are multitudes of Bible characters such as Noah, Abraham, Isaac, Joseph, Moses, David, Mary, Peter, Paul, who displayed the purpose and call of God on their lives in their behavior. Each of these individuals displayed unique personality characteristics that were different from other Bible characters. On the other hand, they also displayed similarities, which we will examine throughout this book.

There were also generational lines of people who had particular skills and abilities, as mentioned in Genesis 4:20-22: *"Jabal who is the father of those who dwell in tents and have livestock"* (these would have been predisposed to be ranchers) ... *"Jubal who is the father of those who play the harp and flute"* (these would have been predisposed to be musicians); and verse 22 speaks of *"Tubal-Cain, an instructor in every craftsman in bronze and iron"* (these would have been predisposed to be artisans).

The apostle Paul speaks of seven motivational gifts in Romans 12:3-8.

> *[3] For I say, through the grace given to me, to everyone who is among you, not to think of himself more highly than he ought to think, but to think soberly, as God has dealt to each one a measure of faith. [4] For as we have many members in one body, but all the members do not have the same function, [5] so we, being many, are one body in Christ, and individually members of one another. [6] Having then gifts differing according to the grace that is given to us, let us use them: if prophecy, let us prophesy in proportion to our faith; [7] or ministry, let us use it in our ministering; he who teaches, in teaching; [8] he who exhorts, in exhortation; he who gives,*

with liberality; he who leads, with diligence; he who shows mercy, with cheerfulness.

When these gifts are naturally found within people, they are predisposed to use them in their lives whether they are born again or not. There are numerous places in the scriptures that reveal both the differences and similarities in people. When we understand some of the predictable characteristics in people, it helps us relate to them in a more positive way. My personal belief is that at the heart of Jesus' teaching concerning the Golden Rule ("Do unto others as you would have them do unto you") is His exhortation to us to be more knowledgeable and understanding of human behavior. It is impossible to carry out His challenge unless we are willing to learn about others.

Character Development: The overarching principle of this book

Another area of crucial importance is the area of character development. Character is the outward manifestation of a person's inner thoughts, which are based on that person's spiritual condition. As it says in Proverbs:

For as he thinks within himself, so he is. "Eat and drink," he says to you, but his heart is not with you (Proverbs 23:7). NKJV

There is much more to healthy relationships than just outward behavior. All of us are capable of "faking it" or wearing masks in our interactions with others. If we are going to be sincere in relationships with others, we must recognize that without a spiritual perspective, our approach starts with selfish intent. We subconsciously ask ourselves, *Is this relationship profitable for me?* So character development must include a way to overpower the SELF-ish intent of the sin nature. This can and does happen through spiritual rebirth.

I can testify to this based on personal experience. I grew up in a very dysfunctional situation that included sixteen years of addiction to alcohol and other things that controlled my life. At the time of this writing, it was 36 years ago that I discovered what it meant to have a personal relationship with Christ and to be born anew in the spirit. I suddenly had the power and motivation to overcome the addictions and the SELFish intent of the sin nature. That does not mean I've arrived, but it does mean that I know where the power to overcome resides. It's spiritual power, not willpower. I can't tell you how many times I tried to "will" myself out of my addictions. It doesn't work. I have been able to walk in victory over alcohol for many years.

The bigger issue for me was how I related to others. I think this is true for most of us; we approach relationships from the perspective that our perception of things are right and the other person needs to change their opinion or their way of doing or seeing things. As I discovered God's desire to relate to me as a loving father, the transformation of my relationships to others began to take place. I have a much greater acceptance and appreciation of people than ever before and a special appreciation of the differences we have. Why? Because God accepted me right where I was with all of my shortcomings bad habits and foolish philosophies. It's not a matter of right and wrong approaches and viewpoints so much as it is different viewpoints and approaches. One is not better than the other; they're just different. When people make this discovery for themselves, it is usually a true awakening.

A good part of the focus in this book will be on character development as a means of enhancing God-given personality traits. Developing Christ-likeness is a Christian's goal, and a lifelong process. There are many different tools to help us accomplish this goal. Any instrument that measures personality traits is just a tool, but it can be helpful in understanding those we associate with in life as well as understanding ourselves.

The presentation on personality contained within the pages of this book is by no means the only answer and is not intended to be. However, we have learned through much experience that understanding some of our predictable behavior characteristics has proven to be very helpful in relating to others in a godly manner. We clearly understand that personality characteristics are only the tip of the iceberg. Human beings are much more diverse than anyone will ever discover through scientific efforts. Rather than seeing personality definitions as limiting, allow the information to broaden your perspective of yourself and others.

We must also keep in mind that it is never acceptable to use our personality type as an excuse not to do something. This is one of the potentially negative aspects of studying personality characteristics. The categorizing that takes place in determining one's personality type is self-induced and can actually limit us from making discoveries. For instance, it's convenient to say, "I can't do that; it doesn't suit my personality." We do the same thing with the spiritual gifts described in the book of First Corinthians. This is one of the main reasons why Christians don't evangelize. "That's not my gift!" they say with self-assured conviction. Potentially, you *"....can do all things through Christ who strengthens you"* (Philippians 4:13), , including those things we are not predisposed to do. It's just that you do some things better and more naturally than you do other things. This is one of the amazing transformations that take place when we become Christians and receive the Holy Spirit. We have God the Holy Spirit living inside us. He can supercharge our personality characteristics that seem to be our weaknesses.

Everyone has strengths and weaknesses. If you maintain a biblical perspective, your weaknesses can actually have more potential than your strengths. The Apostle Paul said:

> *But He said to me, "My grace is sufficient for you, for power is perfected in weakness." Therefore, I will most gladly boast all the more about my weaknesses, so that Christ's power may reside in me (2 Corinthians 12:9).*

It's so important for you to understand that when you made a commitment to Christ, the Spirit of God came to reside in you. The power that is perfected in weakness is generated by faith in Christ and His Word.

As I describe the elements of your particular personality type, you will probably relate to it in varying degrees depending on the strength of your preferences. In order to present clear definitions I will be discussing personality types that are extreme polar opposites. You may find yourself anywhere in between.

The Breath of Life

You are the sons of the prophets and of the covenant that God made with your forefathers, saying to Abraham, And in your seed all the families of the earth will be blessed (Acts 3:25).

This is one example of the many places in Scripture that refer to the perpetuation of life being contained within the seed. This verse is referring specifically to the seed that will provide the potential for all of humanity to experience a relationship with God. The person of Jesus Christ was in the seed of Abraham. It wasn't just a physical genetic connection but a spiritual connection as well. God's design for the universe included giving all living things the miraculous ability to reproduce through their seed. Within the seed are the genetic characteristics of the one producing the seed, but in the case of human beings, added to the seed is life breathed by God.

Then the Lord God formed the man out of the dust from the ground and breathed the breath of life into his nostrils, and the man became a living being (Genesis 2:7).

The breath of life includes the very personal part of God's design for each individual and his or her purpose in life. When a potter puts his creation in the kiln, a process called "firing", the heat from the kiln brings about a very slight change in the piece that is uniquely its own, forever. The piece becomes the finished product of the potter. The breath of God makes subtle but significant changes in each unique individual He creates. Even though two people may have similar behavioral characteristics the Breath of God process makes them unique.

Referring back to the 139th Psalm, the passage you read earlier, it describes in vivid detail how we are uniquely designed by God, and how that design includes the purpose for our life and the personality characteristics we will need to carry out that purpose if we choose to do so through obedience to God. Because He created us with free will, it is our task to connect with God spiritually for insight on the purpose for which He has called us and to develop our God-given personality characteristics.

Within the temperament of each individual reside the core needs and basic values of that individual. These core needs and values go beyond the physical needs and include the relational needs each person has that motivate us to do many of the things we do in life. I will cover our core needs in detail in later chapter.

Adaptability and Talents

The temperament/personality characteristics we're born with give us the ability to interact in this world. They contain behavioral tendencies that influence how we adapt, grow, and develop. When we are in an environment that gives us the freedom to act on our basic instincts, we discover that our energy levels remain high and our stress levels are low. The more the environment requires action from us that is alien to our basic instincts, the more pressure and stress we feel. We may have an extremely high level of energy initially as our adrenalin kicks in, but before long exhaustion sets in. People working in the wrong vocation can experience extended periods of high-level stress. Usually a change will have to be made to get relief from the pressure to do things they don't have the natural abilities to do.

Our Ability to Develop

From the time we're born, we naturally work on developing our basic personality instincts. Because we don't live in a "perfect world" which allows us to have our way in everything we do. God has given us the ability to develop personality or temperament characteristics that move beyond our natural instincts. Based on the environment and the length of time we're in that environment, we begin to develop the needed personality tools to go beyond survival mode and become somewhat proficient. There may be "perks" or "punishment" for behaviors exhibited in the environment, and all of these will make a difference in how we approach the development process. Meanwhile, we make choices as we exercise our free will in responding to life's mosaic of environments. The most influential of all environments is that within which we experience personal relationships with others. Herein lies the value of understanding and developing personality or temperament characteristics.

Borrowed Behavior

We all have the ability to change behavior in an instant depending upon the context of the situation. We call it flexibility and adaptability, and hopefully not manipulation for the purpose of our own profit at the expense of others.

As we go through the developmental process, we become more proficient in the various contexts we face. The term I use is "Borrowed Behavior," and it refers to our ability to draw on both our natural and unnatural but developed strengths that are the best fit for whatever situation we face. If we've gone through life making conscious decisions to understand and develop these strengths, it soon becomes quite natural for us to broaden our capabilities in many different circumstances with many different people. Read the four gospels and you will find Jesus drawing on different aspects of His personality for the situation He faced. He could be straight forward and jarring to the religious leaders that came to him with their arguments or He could show great compassion as He sat on a Hill overlooking and wept over their blindness. He used His personality functions to perfection.

If the development of our skills and abilities are not accomplished as a result of environmental pressures and living in survival mode, we will experience levels of confusion that diminish the development of our natural skills and abilities. When we operate from this perspective, we're kind of like an eight cylinder engine using four cylinders to propel us through life: we will not have the necessary horsepower to get through and over some of the difficult experiences we will face. We will also have the tendency to make the same mistakes in life over and over again. With this in mind, the more energy we put into becoming aware of and understanding our God-given skills and abilities, the better we handle life and relationships. If we knowingly choose an appropriate behavior for a given situation, we'll find that our successes increase and our failures diminish. The apostle Paul said something along these lines:

To the weak I became weak, in order to win the weak. I have become all things to all people, so that I may by all means save some. Now I do all this because of the gospel, that I may become a partner in its benefits (1 Corinthians 9:22-23).

This is an example of understanding the value of Borrowed Behavior. Paul was conscious of his environment and relationships and made appropriate behavioral changes to accomplish his goal.

CHAPTER 2

OVERVIEW OF THE BIBLICAL MAN

To begin with, it is important to understand the Bible's perspective on the nature of man. There are many questions we cannot answer, but one thing we know for certain is that we were created in "God's image and likeness" (Genesis 1:26). NKJV

²⁶ Then God said, "Let Us make man in Our image, according to Our likeness;

That thought alone is enough to boggle the mind! I'm neither a scientist nor a theologian, but I do recognize some of the more obvious things about how we function. So I will do my best with the help of the Bible to give an overview of the particular areas as I see them and I will give as much definition as I can. The Apostle Paul's statement in First Thessalonians gives some insight:

Now may the God of peace himself sanctify you completely, and may your whole spirit and soul and body be kept blameless at the coming of our Lord Jesus Christ (1 Thessalonians 5:23). HCSB

Paul speaks of three distinct aspects of man. In the original Greek language of the New Testament, these words are *pneuma*, *psuchē*, and *sōma*: spirit, soul, and body. Even though it's very difficult to articulate where the lines are drawn for each, I do believe we can see the major differences among these three aspects of the makeup of human nature.

Body

In order that we may interact with the world around us, our body gives us our senses. We have the ability to see, smell, taste, feel, and hear. These five elements give us the ability to experience the physical aspects of our world. We are so marvelously created that if we lose one of our senses, the others can be trained to compensate to a certain degree. All of our senses give us information that is translated into likes and dislikes, danger and safety, splendor and awe, and so on.

Soul

When we consider the soul in relation to how we interact with the world, things aren't quite as clear. The three major areas of the soul are the mind, emotions, and will. Each of these areas is quite complex and will be elaborated on throughout the book. For now I will just give an overview of each of these aspects of the soul.

The following overview is not intended to be an extensive look at the nature of man and the mechanics of the mind but I have purposely kept it as simple as possible that you may see the big picture as quickly as possible. Our mind is our control center. We will consider three aspects of the mind: the conscious mind, the subconscious, and the repressed or unconscious mind.

Our conscious mind has to do with whatever we're experiencing at any given moment. We perceive or see things in either of two ways. We perceive with our five *Senses*, and we perceive *Intuitively*. When we perceive with our five *Senses*, we are dealing with something tangible: we see it, smell it, taste it, feel it, or hear it. Whatever we perceive with our five senses is in the realm of reality. When we perceive *Intuitively*, however, we start with our five senses and proceed on to include other information that may connect with the tangible and expand the meaning of this new information. Many times this sparks ideas and gets the creative juices flowing. I will be expounding on this in later chapters.

As we gather information through our perceptive functions, we quickly turn to judging the information. We draw conclusions as to whether the information is helpful or unhelpful, important or unimportant, worth remembering or forgettable, dangerous or delightful, and so on. There are also two ways to judge. One is called *Thinking*, which takes a very objective approach to the conclusions it reaches. *Thinking* involves evaluating the facts, the truth, principles, logic, and so on. Another way to evaluate is called *Feeling*. Don't confuse this type of feeling with the emotional responses we have because it is a rational process just as *Thinking* is a rational process, but when someone prefers to use the *Feeling* process for decision-making, they take a much more subjective approach. *Feelers* evaluate the information subjectively; they are concerned with how this new information affects family, friends, and themselves. Life is about people and relationships.

Our subconscious mind has to do with our ability to store information and experiences. We can draw on our sub-conscious mind at will and bring the stored information and experience into the area of the conscious. This is our memory. It seems as though the younger you are, the greater percentage of memory is recallable. Of course, as we age there are a lot more bits of information and experiences stored. Like our computer hard drive, sometimes the memories get "fragmented" and it takes longer to gather the data. Our emotions can be attached to information and experiences in our memories as well. This is why we can give thought to a lost loved one, for instance, and re-experience grief, or on a different note, we can relive that amazing first-place finish and experience the jubilation we felt once again. The Bible has much to say about our thoughts.

The repressed or unconscious section of our mind relates to the incredible ability we have to repress or subdue memories of experiences and information. This usually takes place after receiving shocking information or having a traumatic experience. We can go through life never giving thought to the information or experiences that we have repressed. We repress things we don't know how to process when the fear or insecurity is overwhelming. I don't have a lot of patience for those who brush off this explanation of repression as mere psycho-babble. This is an extreme way of looking at things, and it is unrealistic in that it totally negates the ability to minister to someone who is struggling in life because of traumatic experiences. However, I also don't have a lot of patience with people who refuse to take responsibility for their own decisions and instead blame everyone and everything for their behavior or situation. This is also extreme thinking, in that it blocks the power of the Cross as well as its ability to accomplish emotional healing in one's life. My wife and I have worked with people for the last thirty years in pastoral counseling who have experienced a lot of emotional pain without realizing where it was coming from, only to experience a touch from the Holy Spirit that gave not only revelation but healing as well.

Emotions

Our emotions have a direct impact on the quality of life we experience. Our emotions respond to experiences and thoughts, and these responses can be good or bad. Our emotions can warn us of impending danger or give us feelings of elation. We can empathize with others and relate to their experiences through our emotions. That is why it is so important to have a positive outlook on life. Even when we have bad experiences and a corresponding negative emotional reaction, we can override the emotion with perspective. This is why the Apostle Paul said in Romans 5:3-5:

> [3] *And not only that, but we also glory in tribulations, knowing that tribulation produces perseverance; and perseverance,* [5]*character; and character, hope. Now hope does not disappoint, because the love of God has been poured out in our hearts by the Holy Spirit who was given to us. NKJV*

James the brother of Jesus had the same exhortation for the 1st century followers of Christ when he said in James 1:2-4:

> [2] *My brethren, count it all joy when you fall into various trials, knowing that the testing of your faith produces patience. But*

let patience have its perfect work, that you may be perfect and complete, lacking nothing. NKJV

These words by Paul and James are intended to get followers of Christ to live life at the level God intended. God will always be there if we allow Him to be, but the choice is ours. Living a life of faith will always present us with the positive side of life and encourage us to rejoice in the midst of trials and tribulation.

Will

I consider our will our moral agent. It is the trigger to our actions, both good and bad. It determines the direction we take; it is the ultimate decision maker. The decisions are calculated with the help of all aspects of our mind and emotions, and the will is our moment of truth that reveals what we're made of, what our philosophy of life really is, and what our convictions really are. We do what we believe. This is actually a biblical principle. The key, however, is to believe rightly, and when you do, right actions will follow. As James said:

But be doers of the word, and not hearers only, deceiving yourselves (James 1:22) NKJV

The deception James speaks of has to do with anything that is in opposition to God's Word, whether it is rooted in the mind or the emotions. Here's where the influence of the sin nature and the spiritual forces of darkness come into play. It's the point of temptation where we have a choice to make: Will we do things God's way or our way? Once again in James 1:12-15 James explains the process:

[12] Blessed is the man who endures temptation; for when he has been approved, he will receive the crown of life which the Lord has promised to those who love Him. Let no one say when he is tempted, "I am tempted by God"; for God cannot be tempted by evil, nor does He Himself tempt anyone. But each one is tempted when he is drawn away by his own desires and enticed. Then, when desire has conceived, it

gives birth to sin; and sin, when it is full-grown, brings forth death. NKJV

This is why Paul says we're to "take every thought captive" (2 Corinthians 10:3-6).

3 For although we are walking in the flesh, we do not wage war in a fleshly way, since the weapons of our warfare are not fleshly, but are powerful through God for the demolition of strongholds. We demolish arguments and every highminded thing that is raised up against the knowledge of God, taking every thought captive to the obedience of Christ. And we are ready to punish any disobedience, once your obedience is complete. HCSB

Our will is the trigger that determines our next step – whether we walk down the narrow path or the wide path.

Spirit

The function of our spirit is dependent upon whether it has experienced re-birth or not. Before we have faith in Jesus Christ's redemption of our sins through His death, burial, and resurrection, we are spiritually dead. Our spirit is dormant. Our flesh has complete control of our life. We remain controlled by our sin nature that we inherited from our father Adam. We have no spiritual understanding; we cannot communicate with God outside of the prayer of surrender. The future is dark, especially when eternity is considered. However, when a person comes to a place in their life where the Holy Spirit has convicted them of sin, righteousness, and judgment, as Jesus said would happen, (John 16:7-8):

7 Nevertheless, I am telling you the truth. It is for your benefit that I go away, because if I don't go away the Counselor will not come to you. If I go, I will send Him to you. When He comes, He will convict the world about sin, righteousness, and judgment: HCSB and they surrender to God as a result of this conviction, a marvelous miracle takes place. They are "born again" and their spirit is in-dwelt by the Holy Spirit, and they begin to lead and direct their life in the will of God. Our born-again spirit is the part of us that wants to do the will of God. It has the ability to understand spiritual things because it's no longer dormant but is alive in Christ. The Bible comes alive, and communication with God is a moment-by-moment experience. Why would anyone want it any other way? Our purpose and fulfillment in life on this earth can finally be realized once we are born again.

In this section, we will examine some of the personality characteristics that aid us in exemplifying Christ-like behavior. I want to emphasize that these personality traits are simply tools that give us the ability to function on this planet. This becomes clear as we look at the Myers-Briggs Type Indicator. How we use these tools determines how we develop Christ-like character.

It would not be necessary for us to understand personality dynamics if we lived and behaved as Jesus did while He walked on earth. My experience, however, is that the vast majority of Christians don't live as Jesus lived, especially when it comes to handling relationships in a way that glorifies the Father. Therefore, we need every tool we can find that will help us accomplish the goal of becoming Christ-like. That's what this book is about. When it's all said and done and we are standing before the Lord, we will want Him to say to us, *"Well done, good and faithful servant."* (Matt.25:12) But He will only say that if we've impacted others' lives in a way that has infused them with health and wholeness. As far as Jesus is concerned, the only thing that matters while we're on this planet is what we've done to impart life to those with whom we come in contact.

It is my prayer that this book will go a long way toward helping you accomplish this goal. Make a commitment to read and reread where necessary to become an expert in recognizing, understanding, and appreciating the measurable differences we see in others.

Holly Brook Baptist Church
3219 S. FM 2869
Hawkins, TX 75765-4732

CHAPTER 3

OVERVIEW OF THE MYERS–BRIGGS TYPE INDICATOR

This chapter will present a brief overview of the Myers-Briggs because I do not want to spend a lot of time in this book discussing theory. However, I will provide enough information so that you will have a basic understanding of how the theory works. For a broader understanding of the theory, I suggest reading the book *Gifts Differing* by Isabel Briggs Myers, with Peter B. Myers.[3] The other thing I would like to point out is that you're about to learn a new language: the language of the Myers-Briggs Personality Theory. Because it has its own unique terminology, I consider this the most important chapter in the book. You will probably have to come back to this chapter to clarify some of the definitions from time to time, and I believe it is a worthwhile endeavor to do so. The words I use to describe various aspects of a personality will soon become second nature to you. But you must push through anything that is difficult to understand at first and gain a good comprehension of this chapter.

One of the reasons Linda and I gravitated towards the Myers-Briggs is because the theory is easily visible in the behavior of people. Everyone gathers information and then evaluates that infor-

---

[3] *Gifts Differing*, Isabel Briggs Myers, with Peter B. Myers, Consulting Psychologists Press, Inc.

mation. The word that the Myers-Briggs theory uses to describe these two processes is the *Functions*. I believe this is the heart of the Myers-Briggs theory. Functions are the processes we use to cope with all that we encounter in life. As I describe the areas of our personality, it is important to make careful note of the terminology used for describing each characteristic. To help with this I will capitalize and place in italics the words that identify key aspects of the Myers-Briggs terminology. Refer to Illustration 6 as I describe these characteristics.

The Four Functions of Personality

Lets take a look at the Functions available to every individual.

The heart of the Myers Brigs rests on two main Functions called Perceiving and Judging. These Functions describe how we gather data and how we evaluate data. We gather and evaluate lightening fast and don't give thought to which Function we are using at the time. (Most people are totally unaware) We do prefer one Function above the other but all four are available and are used by each individual to varying degrees.

The Perceiving Functions

The Two Perceiving Functions Are Called:

Sensing		Intuition
(Gathers data with the five senses. This is tangible, concrete data. Black and white)		(Gathers data through hunches, gut feelings and ideas. Intangible, grey areas)

Next we look at the Judging Functions:

The Judging Functions

The Two Judging Functions Are Called:

Thinking	Feeling
(Evaluates data objectively, looking for facts, truth, logic, cause and effect)	(Evaluates data subjectively, asking how will the data impact, themselves and others)

The *Perceiving* functions are *Sensing* (S) and *Intuition* (N) and the *Judging* functions are *Thinking* (T) and *Feeling* (F). By the way, when I use the term Judge that is exactly what I mean. We all make judgments on the information we gather. Don't confuse the terms *Judge* or *Judging* with being judgmental. The word judge is not a negative term. It is also important to note that the Judging function termed *Feeling* does not relate to an emotional decision-making process based on one's feelings. *Feeling* as a Judging function, is a cognitive or mental process. I will cover this topic in more detail in chapter six.

Everyone uses all four functions in their daily lives, but each of us prefers one type to another. We use the functions to varying degrees. We use both Sensing and Intuition to gather information, and then we use Thinking and Feeling to evaluate that information. However, we always prefer or trust one function over the other. My own preference for gathering information is Sensing. I trust that process for gathering information more than I trust Intuition. I do use Intuition when I use my imagination, or when I make a connection with other information that isn't currently before me, or when I exercise faith, for that matter. But for the most part I trust something if I can see it, taste it, feel it, smell it, or hear it. The person who prefers the Intuitive function will never take the tangible at face value; they believe there is always more than meets the eye. For the Judging process, I prefer Thinking rather than Feeling. I like to make my decisions based on fact, truth, logic, and principles. I take a very objective approach to decision making. However, I have learned to use the Feeling function when making decisions that include sensitive relationship issues. The Judging process of Feeling is more subjective in its appraisal of any given situation. Someone who is a Feeler asks the question, *What kind of impact will this information have on others and on me?* Those who tend to use the Feeling function conclude that compassion or empathy is needed in any given situation, or a strong stance is needed to protect what is valuable. As stated in chapter one, we can develop the functions that aren't our natural tendencies, and doing so will expand our ability to Perceive and Judge, which in turn will inject more balance into everything we do. These personality functions can be developed unconsciously because of pressures or situations we must adapt to in our environment, or they can be developed consciously as we discover how to go about increasing our ability to use a particular function. In fact, sometimes we're uncertain of our strongest function simply because of the environment we're in. This is especially true when a child is not allowed the freedom to discover his or her natural abilities in the early years of life, but the development of any of the functions can be impacted by our environment.

In our adult years we will have a tendency to gravitate toward environments that are more naturally suited to our preferred functions. When Linda and I were on staff at a major university, we met a young man who was a business major. He was from another country, and his parents had given him only a few choices about his major: business, engineering, medicine, or law. Unfortunately, he didn't have any internal motivation for any of those vocations. He struggled but worked hard and graduated with his business major. As he pursued a position in the business world, he continued to fail miserably. Eventually he took some additional courses directing him towards a vocation that felt right to him. He has been successful in the pursuits that were of his own choosing. Sometimes we parents tend to push our children toward a career goal that is more suited for us and not our child. We cannot forcefully make our child a "chip off the old block." This is another reason we should put some effort into learning about personality differences. We make much better parents when we have some insight into the inborn preferences of our children.

Sensing – S

In the results of your personality assessment, Sensing will be identified with a capitol S. Sensing is exactly what it sounds like: taking information in with your five senses. It's what you see, smell, taste, hear, and feel. We all do these things. We're capable of distinguishing colors, tasting different flavors, smelling different aromas, feeling different textures, and seeing everything before us. The person that prefers to use Sensing as their primary way to gather information is highly aware of their surroundings. They have a very literal way of viewing the world, and there are very little if any "gray areas" in the way they gather information. Such gray areas (which are actually preferred by Intuitives) are considered unstable ground by those who are Sensors. Sensors are aware of all the details in their data-gathering process. Sensors are also good with short-term goals; they live in the here and now and are very efficient within that framework. However, this hinders their ability to see the big picture, because for Sensors, the big picture is built piece by piece and not conceptually.

Intuition – N

In the results of your personality assessment, Intuition will be identified with a capitol N. (Capitol "I" is already used for Introversion) People who prefer Intuition in their approach to gathering information may or may not start with Sensing but will then move quickly to Intuition as ideas and hunches begin to take over and give birth to possibilities. Their vivid imagination opens the door to new ways of doing things both relationally and mechanically depending on their primary Judging function. Someone who primarily uses Intuition brings forth ideas and creativity. Intuition sees what might be. Most of what Intuitives perceive is in the gray area where change is always possible, and they tend to avoid the approach preferred by Sensors, who see things more realistically and with clearly drawn lines of demarcation, which seems like a much too restrictive way of perceiving to the Intuitive. Another aspect of Intuitives is that they are future oriented in reference to time. The Intuitive can be good with long-term goals. An Intuitive sees the big picture but sometimes has difficulty with the details.

Thinking – T

In the results of your personality assessment, Thinking will be identified with a capitol T. People who prefer Thinking instead of Feeling when making decisions place a high value on objectivity. They filter information through principles, facts, truth, and logic. Their decision-making focus is directive and corrective rather than relational. Thinkers struggle with the idea of placing their personal values ahead of what seems to be the facts or truth.

Feeling – F

In the results of your personality assessment, Feeling will be identified with a capitol F. People who prefer Feeling in their decision-making process place a high value on subjectivity. Everything is about values and relationships to them. Their value system is built around the important things in life. A driving internal question that motivates their decisions is, *How is this information going to impact me and my family or friends?* Feelers struggle with making decisions based solely on the facts available to them or based on what is considered the truth.

My wife Linda and I are opposites in this regard. I am a Thinker and she is a Feeler. If we went house hunting together, I would be considering things such as the cost of the house, whether the mortgage payment will fit into the family budget, the amount of maintenance the house will require, the condition of the roof, any improvements that might be needed, and so on. Linda would want to know if the dining room was large enough for a table that would seat the entire family at Thanksgiving; if there was at least one extra bedroom for houseguests; whether or not the house has a warm and cozy feeling to it, and so on.

The Four Personality Attitudes

The preceding section discussed very briefly the four personality functions. The two perceiving-type functions are *Sensing* and *Intuition*. The two judging-type functions are *Thinking* and *Feeling*. As mentioned previously, we use all four functions, but our most trusted perceiving and judging functions work for us most of the time.

The four functions are impacted by four personality attitudes. The first two we're going to examine are the attitudes of *Extraversion* and *Introversion*. In my experience, there is a lot of misunderstanding about the behavioral characteristics of *Extraverts* and *Introverts*. Please read the next two descriptions carefully (and you may even need to go back and read them again; that's quite all right). It's important to have a thorough understanding of these definitions.

Attitude Number One

These Two Attitudes Are Called:

Introversion	Extraversion
(When you prefer to take the Functions internally)	(When you prefer to interact externally with the Functions)

The Extraverted Attitude – E

In the results of your personality assessment, Extraversion will be identified with a capitol E. Extraversion is a preference for interacting with the outer world. An Extravert has a predisposition for processing externally with their dominant function, which is their preferred function (dominant), and processing internally with their auxiliary function, which is their second most preferable function. Since Extraverts use their dominant function when interacting with others, they derive energy from being around people or being involved in activities that require the gathering together of people. They process information and or conclusions externally depending on what they prefer as a dominant function. In fact Extraverts clarify their thoughts as they interact with others. Later on, we will discuss in detail how to determine your first (dominant), second (auxiliary), third, and fourth functions.

The Introverted Attitude – I

In the results of your personality assessment, Introversion will be identified with a capital I. Introversion is an attitude that prefers to mull over their Perceptions and Judgments internally. An Introvert will have a predisposition for processing externally with their auxiliary function, which is their second most preferable function, and will process internally using their dominant function, which is their favorite function. This process is the opposite of that used by the Extravert. This preference has a bearing on how much they interact with the external world. Introverts derive energy from being alone. Processing information and reaching conclusions internally using their dominant function requires spending most of their time in the internal world. It makes sense, then, that Introverts may appear to be loners, and in most cases, Introverts are quieter than Extraverts until you get on a subject that they have adequately thought through and enjoy talking about.

In the next chapter, we will take a more detailed look at the differences between Extraverts and Introverts.

Preface to the Final Two Aspects of Personality Differences

As we look at these next two attitudes, it will seem as though I'm being redundant with the terminology. Please don't get frustrated here. Stick with me and it will soon come together. One is called the Judging attitude and one is called the Perceiving attitude. This last attitude is describing and more accurately pointing back to the particular function you use while interacting with the external world. As you will see when we continue on, these last two attitudes give an outward, visible definition of who we are to the people with whom we interact.

Attitude Number Two

These Two Attitudes Are Called:

Judging	Perceiving
(Says you Extravert your Judging Function and impacts on your behavior as such; Closure, Time Oriented, & Structure)	(Says you Extravert your Perceiving Function and impacts on your behavior as such; Open-ended, Unaware of time, Unstructured)

Let me use the four-letter combination of my own personality to help clarify how these work together. I am an **ESTJ**. What does this tell me about my personality?

E says I'm Extraverted. This means that the primary way I recharge my internal batteries, so to speak, is by spending time with other people.

S means that I prefer to gather data using the function of Sensing. In other words, I'm a realist.

T means that I prefer to come to conclusions about data by using the function of Thinking. I'm objective with my decisions (as opposed to subjective).

J means that I will interact with the external world primarily with my Judging function (T). People will mostly hear about the conclusions I've come to.

I could give a lot more examples of what each letter signifies in terms of behavior, but this will be discussed in more depth later. I want to run through the definitions again using the four letters that would be my mirror opposite.

I denotes someone who is Introverted. This means that the primary way they recharge their internal batteries, so to speak, is by being alone.

N denotes someone who prefers to use the function of Intuition to gather data. This person is creative and is motivated by changes, new ideas, and possibilities.

F denotes someone who prefers to use the function of Feeling to make conclusions about the data they gather. This person is more subjective in their decision-making process.

P denotes someone who interacts with the external world primarily with his or her Perceiving function. People will hear mostly about the ideas and vision for the future I have.

Each letter of your type gives some definition to your personality characteristics and at the same time interacts with the other letters. When you realize that you use the characteristics to varying degrees, your personal uniqueness comes to the forefront. With this little bit of information you can quickly see that the **ESTJ** person and the **INFP** person are going to behave very differently. You will see how differently as you progress through this book.

As mentioned previously, each of us uses all four functions, but how frequently and when we use them depends on how comfortable we are using the third and fourth functions in particular.

As an **ESTJ**, I'm aware that my least frequently used function is Feeling. If my dominant is Thinking it would be used most by me. That means my Feeling function is the least used. The Feeling function is the particular function that is essential in the context of ministry. For instance, when someone is in pain because of a loss, compassion and empathy are needed. My natural tendency as a Thinker *(my d*ominant function) would be to direct them to a resolution to their problem, or to find a way to "fix it" for them, which of course is impossible when someone is grieving. More than anything, they need a listening ear or maybe even to be held while they weep. Early on in ministry, I was oblivious to the Feeling function and tried to fix all of the difficulties that arose in people's lives. Linda, whose secondary function is Feeling, helped me a lot in this area. Your third and fourth functions sometimes lay dormant and need to be recognized, and a conscious effort needs to be made to develop them.

If you've completed the personality assessment, this would be a good time to look at your four letters and define them as I have done here, and then ask yourself if you are developing your third and fourth functions. Knowing the order and definition of each of the four functions will help you understand what you need to develop in any particular environment.

The Judging Attitude – J

In the results of your personality assessment, Judging will be identified with a capital **J**. The person who scores J on their assessment will approach the external world with the conclusions they've come to. Once they have decided how things should be, they get to work organizing their world. Of course, all of that organization requires time, and there seems to be an internal clock built into the person who prefers **J** as an Attitude. With all of the J's decision-making, sometimes they are accused of reaching premature conclusions and being too narrow-minded in their viewpoints.

The Perceiving Attitude – P

In the results of your personality assessment, Perceiving will be identified with a capital **P**. The person who scores **P** on their assessment will approach the external world with their newly gathered information. When they make new discoveries, they are excited about letting others know about them. Of course, with so much information gathering, the **P** isn't focused on concluding there is more Perceiving to do. Therefore, sometimes the P is accused of being a procrastinator.

In this chapter, we have taken a brief look at what's behind the Myers-Briggs personality definitions. A deeper study of the Myers-Briggs functions, also known as mental or cognitive processes, would reveal that in this book we're only touching the surface of the amount of information available. My purpose and goal is not to make you an expert on the Myers-Briggs but to put a tool in your hand that will help you become better at developing quality relationships. Understanding the basics of the Myers-Briggs will help you get the most out of this book.

CHAPTER 4

COMPARING THE TWO ATTITUDES OF INTROVERSION AND EXTRAVERSION

To give more clarity regarding the comparisons in the following four chapters I will use various examples from the lives of people we know who have shared their experiences with us. Some stories will come from our own lives as well. We are different in two of the four areas, and if you consider how I score very close on Extraversion and Introversion, and Linda is undoubtedly an Extravert, many times we behave as if we're different in this area as well. Once again, my four letters are ESTJ and Linda's are ESFP. Before I get started on comparing the opposite attitudes of Extraverts or Introverts, I first need to offer an explanation. This will also give you some insight into the fact that you cannot look at just one of the letters in your type and learn all there is to learn about that particular trait. Each letter of your type is interwoven into the others and at different dimensions as well.

Some people score very close on Extraversion and Introversion, and in my case, I operate like an Extravert when I'm in any environment that requires production and processes such as manufacturing or sales, and I operate more like an Introvert when I'm in an environment that requires a lot of interaction with people, especially helping people, such as counseling or social service work. I consistently score right in the middle of these two attitudes, so I might flip-flop more than someone who scores stronger in only one, whether Introversion or Extraversion. The reason it works this way for me is because my dominant function is that of Thinking, and my fourth function is Feeling. Most Sensing Thinkers are happy and more energized in vocations that require performance, production, and processes. You will find that both Sensing Feelers and Intuitive Feelers are happy and more energized in vocations that require a lot of interaction with people, especially if it is harmonious interaction. When we compare the functions of Thinking and Feeling, I will elaborate some more on this topic.

As we examine each of these traits, we will answer two vital questions that bring us down to the level of our daily lives: *What impact does this trait have on relationships?* Second, challenge yourself to make some improvements by finishing this statement: *What can (Extroverts; Introverts; Feelers, and so on) do to improve their relationships?*

Following these exercises will be *Life Application Verses* that relate to the specific experience of each personality trait. These Bible verses speak directly to the particular aspects of these personality traits. It is essential for us to examine these topics in light of Scripture. Our goal as Christians is clearly stated in the book of Romans:

Be transformed by the renewing of your mind, so that you may discern what is the good, pleasing, and perfect will of God (Romans 12:2b).

Let me offer another reminder as I begin: one preference is no better than another preference; it is just different. We diminish our full potential when we fake it to make it while trying to fit in or win someone's acceptance. Learn to appreciate and accept who God created you to be, and walk in that freedom. When we assume we have to be a certain way in order to be accepted by others, we enter into a form of bondage that short circuits God's plan for our lives. The more important approach to life is being consistent in our efforts to provide ministry to those we meet along the way.

Strengths and Weaknesses

There is something very important to keep in mind as you look at comparing these personality traits: When **pushed to an extreme, your strengths become weaknesses.** Learning where to draw the line with any of your preferences will improve your relationships. For example, Extraverts easily and assuredly use their natural verbal skills to communicate with others. This is a positive trait, but if the Extravert has the tendency to dominate conversations, people will begin to shy away from him or her. Interaction with others is a two-way street, and nobody wants to sit and listen to someone go on and on without taking a breath.

The Introvert who never contributes to a conversation becomes a source of frustration to the people they are in relationship with. Introverting your thoughts and conclusions is a positive way to bring clarity to your viewpoints, but if you never share your viewpoints, people will begin to wonder if you have any viewpoints, or they may wonder if you even like them.

If you learn to recognize your tendencies to push your strengths (which are like blind spots) to an extreme, it will improve your relationships with all of your family and friends.

Determining Your Personality Preferences (your four-letter combination)

In the following sections, you will notice that under each numbered title there are two descriptions, one for each of the opposite attitudes and functions being discussed in that section. There is a box next to these descriptions. After you have read the descriptions and the additional examples, come back to the boxes and put a tick mark in the box that best describes you.

Over the years, we have found this is a more accurate way to determine your type than answering questions on a questionnaire. When answering a questionnaire it is very hard to determine your natural preferences in particular environments such as work, school, or family. Reading through the descriptions and examples of each attitude and function should help to clarify which one is your preference. Remember, there are no right or wrong answers, no best way or worst way to function. This whole process involves making discoveries about your actual preferences and not about what you think you should be or what others may be asking or expecting of you regarding your behavior.

1. Extraverts and Introverts: How They Direct Their Energy

- ☐ The **Extravert** is energized by being with others and by having much involvement in activities. Extraverts suffer energy loss when they are isolated from people and activities for an extended period.

- ☐ The **Introvert** is energized from their time spent alone, and conversely from the Extravert, the Introvert suffers energy loss when they are involved with people and external activities for extended periods.

Insights on Extraversion

What impact does this trait have on relationships?

When an Introvert interacts with people all day long, thus have been Extraverting, they need to spend some time throughout the day Introverting for a while to regain energy. If an introvert works in a position that requires a lot of interaction with others it would be good for them to get away from people during their breaks and even retreat during their lunch periods. They will come back somewhat refreshed. If they continue to interact even casually during these breaks they will begin to feel it as the day progresses and by the end of the day will definitely need some alone time.

On the other hand, if an Extravert spends most of their day at home they begin to feel tired or may even experience mild depression. When the spouse or roommate gets home from work they will hear the details of the Extraverts day. For Extraverts who are homemakers or if they work out of their homes getting out for a walk or errands a couple of times a day and mixing with friends or even with the general population is important and it will help them maintain their energy levels.

When couples recognize and adapt to each other's needs concerning personality characteristics, it improves their marriage considerably. It is important for me to give Linda some talk time or time out in public. She also realizes as that I need to be re-energized from my day of Extraverting by taking a short nap. It's okay to do that Introverts!

What can Extraverts do to improve their relationships?

If you are an Extravert and your spouse is an Introvert, allow them to have some time alone when he or she needs it; protect that time from intrusion by anyone, including those who call on the phone.

Life application verse:

Everyone should look out not only for his own interests, but also for the interests of others. (Philippians 2:4 HCSB).

Insights on Introversion

What impact does this trait have on relationships?

Being in the ministry for thirty-plus years has given me an appreciation of Introversion and how much it's helped me when it comes to study, prayer, and meditation. I have learned to guard my opportunities to gain alone time. When it comes to relationships however, Introverts must push beyond their internal desire to withdraw and make a decision to learn the value and appreciate their time with others. It will pay tremendous dividends.

In the ministry, I sometimes find myself exhausted because of all the people and communication requirements that come along with serving others. As a result, I can sometimes be too abrupt in my communication, which causes misunderstandings to happen. I'm not anti-social or angry when I speak abruptly to people; it's simply because I am just physically tired and need to recharge my batteries with some alone time.

What can Introverts do to improve their relationships?

Understanding how you use your four functions will help you see the impact of Introversion and Extraversion on your relationships. Sensing will help you tune into the moment and not drift, help you with compliments and affirmation concerning clothes, hair etc., Intuition will help you pick up on the nuances such as body language, facial expressions, and read between the lines in the conversation. Thinking will help you with an intellectual conversation, even if it's just asking questions which helps show an interest, Feeling helps you bring comfort and care and sincerity to the individual your communicating with. All the while you are applying Extraversion and Introversion as needed. I challenge you to practice this method from time to time and see how much it helps you recognize the four functions.

Another important area for Introverts is knowing when you've reached your limits. Freely admit when you're tired and need to withdraw. Exercise in order to stay in good physical condition, which helps combat exhaustion. Try to get enough sleep, and consciously draw on the power of the Holy Spirit during times of extended interaction with the external world.

Life application verse:

> *I am able to do all things through Him who strengthens me (Philippians 4:13 HCSB).*

2. Boundaries: The Difference between Extraverts and Introverts

- ☐ The **Extravert** can be a space invader. I'm not talking about intergalactic space travel! I'm talking about personal space. For the Extravert, there seem to be no boundaries when it comes to their interactions with other people.

- ☐ The **Introvert** will set and respect boundaries. He or she actually needs to be invited into your space.

Insights on Extraversion

What impact does this trait have on relationships?

Extraverts love to be involved with people. When they attend a social event, it doesn't take too long to join into a group conversation and begin interacting with the people very freely and openly. Most of the time it works out well and they end up with new friends. Occasionally they may end up getting involved in what was meant to be a private conversation, and that can be embarrassing.

What can Extraverts do to improve their relationships?

An Extravert should make an effort to be more sensitive to what's going on in a group conversation before jumping in. When they're in a group setting, they also need to be aware of the Introverts standing outside of the group who need to be invited into the conversation. An Extravert can also be more sensitive to Introverts who "internalize" their thoughts, and can ask to have a moment of their time before just assuming they want to be drawn into conversation with the Extravert.

Life application verse:

A passerby who meddles in a quarrel that's not his is like one who grabs a dog by the ears (Proverbs 26:17 HCSB).

Insights on Introversion

What impact does this trait have on relationships?

If an Introvert is not required to interact, especially in a situation where they don't know anyone, they are perfectly content not to interact. The downside to this is that they can appear to be shy or timid, or even aloof and distant; but more importantly, they can miss opportunities to expand their world by getting to know people they've never met before.

What can Introverts do to improve their relationships?

Introverts have to make a decision to expend the energy to get to know people and to take an interest in developing relationships with them. It is a choice that must be made, and for the most part, they'll find that developing new relationships is a blessing when the effort has been put forth.

People are put in our path for a purpose, usually one that relates to our ongoing ministry as Christians. Sometimes this has to do with introducing them to Christ, and sometimes it has to do with providing them with some element of God-given and directed ministry.

Life application verse:

> *Now everything is from God, who reconciled us to Himself through Christ and gave us the ministry of reconciliation (2 Corinthians 5:18 HCSB).*

3. Taking the Initiative in Relationships

- ☐ The **Extravert** is good at meeting new people. They will usually make the first move.

- ☐ The **Introvert** may avoid meeting new people, and usually waits for others to make the move.

Insights on Extraversion

What impact does this trait have on relationships?

Extraverts develop relationships with others by making the first move. Therefore they normally have more friends than Introverts. Extraverts relationships with others may not be as deep as the Introverts who have fewer friends. The Extravert seems to be tuned in to the people that are in their immediate vicinity, for example;

An Extravert can be at a theme park or the County Fair and will go use the public restroom and when they come out, invariably they're not alone. At first glance they seem to be talking to a friend like they are long lost buddies. When the friend departs and you ask them, *"Who was that,"* there response is *"Oh, I didn't get the name."* Extraverts interact with others very quickly and easily and it is especially true if they are Extraverted and a Feeler. With this in mind the Extravert will usually have a lot of friends.

Insights on Introversion

What impact does this trait have on relationships?

Introverts will have fewer friends than the Extravert, but chances are the depth of their relationships goes deeper than that of the Extravert. The Introvert lives in a smaller world than does the Extravert because of what each and every relationship brings us throughout our lives. Meeting one more person will impact your life to some degree. Much of life is about networking with others and for a myriad of reasons but Introverts don't network very well.

What can Introverts do to improve their relationships?

I have good friends who are Introverted Pastors. In the ministry they have learned to make the first move especially on Sunday mornings and especially with people who are new to the church. Of course, this is a very friendly environment so that helps and usually people would like to meet the pastor so initiating in this situation is pretty easy. But the feedback I get is that by doing so they have also learned methods that help them become more initiating in all of their relationships.

I will assert myself in social situations. I have found that new relationships add new opportunities to give and receive, not to mention the new flavor life takes on with every new relationship.

Life application verse:

> *"A friend loves at all times, and a brother is born for adversity." (Proverbs 17:17 HCSB)*

4. Openness in Relationships

- ☐ The **Extravert** shows the world who they are; thus, there are few surprises with an Extravert.

- ☐ The **Introvert** has an important hidden side. They reveal a little of themselves at a time to trusted friends.

Insights on Extraversion

What impact does this trait have on relationships?

Extraverts like free-flowing conversations. Information is to be communicated, not kept to themselves and pondered over as Introverts tend to do. Quite often, an Extravert's life is an open book. When you first meet an Extravert, you know almost everything about him or her within a short time. Extraverts tend to "fly by the seat of their pants" in a conversation with others, which means they don't always give a lot of thought to what they're going to say next, and they assume others are approaching the conversation the same way. If the other person in the conversation is an Extravert as well, they're probably flowing right along together, sometimes even talking at the same time, and yet they both most likely know the gist of the conversation!

What can Extraverts do to improve their relationships?

Slow down just a bit. There is such a thing as "too much information." Take notice of the words your about to speak, remembering that once a word is spoken you can't get it back. It's better to be a little slower while conversing and bless others than to be quick to speak and accidentally hurt someone with your words.

Life verse for this issue:

When there are many words, sin is unavoidable, but the one who controls his lips is wise (Proverbs 10:19).

Insights on Introversion

What impact does this trait have on relationships?

From an Introvert's perspective, information is to be evaluated and not communicated unless someone asks for it, or if they do want to communicate something they typically won't fight for communication space. Introverts are just as active as Extraverts are at gathering information; however they don't see any reason to share that information unless they're asked for it. They are also very selective regarding the kind of information they do share. If it's personal information, the Introvert generally will not share much of it with anyone except maybe very close friends. So there's a lot more to an Introvert than most people know. When it comes to Introverts, we see only the tip of the iceberg.

What can Introverts do to improve their relationships?

Introverts should take a more assertive approach in sharing their ideas and conclusions. Generally people around you are interested to hear what you have to say. Feel free to preface what you have to say, for example, *"can I contribute something to this conversation?"* or *"excuse me, can I say something"* then proceed. Usually prefacing will get everyone's attention and you'll have fewer interruptions.

An Introvert will be open to sharing things they normally consider private, if doing so is for the greater goal of helping others cope, or helping them overcome things they might be struggling with. An Introvert will give input at brainstorming sessions without having to feel the information release is premature and has not been evaluated fully and conclusions drawn.

Life application verse:

> Lord, open my lips, and my mouth will declare Your praise (Psalm 51:15 HCSB).

5. Styles of Communication

- ☐ The **Extravert** is good at the give-and-take of fast, spontaneous conversations.

- ☐ The **Introvert** prefers a slower pace in conversation, choosing to carefully weigh what they're about to say.

Insights on Extraversion

What impact does this trait have on relationships?

This is a major communication issue. If you're an Extravert and you have an issue you need to discuss with someone, you typically want to jump right in to the communication process and talk it through. The Extravert feels like everyone should be able to just throw it out there, so to speak, and talk through an issue – even important issues – on the run. If it involves historical information, such as asking about something that was previously discussed, it usually isn't a problem for the Introvert to give a quick response, but if it involves new information, the Introvert usually prefers to have some time to think it through.

What can Extraverts do to improve their relationships?

The first thing an Extravert needs to do is determine whether they're communicating with another Extravert or an Introvert. When they know they're dealing with an Introvert, especially concerning a difficult topic, the Extravert should simply communicate their concerns and ask if the two of them can get together at a prescribed time and discuss the issue. Pressing the Introvert for an immediate answer will bring a lot of added stress to the situation and maybe even cause inaccurate information.

If an Extravert needs an answer or input immediately, they might preface what they're asking for by saying something like, *"I need your quick input on something, but right now I'm just gathering ideas. What do you think about such-and-such?"* The Introvert will probably take some time to think it through even if an Extravert prefaces the request for information in this manner. Thus, the Extravert should ask the Introvert to get back to you if they have further thoughts on the matter. With a little time to think things through in their own time, the Introvert surely will.

Life application verse:

> *Do nothing out of rivalry or conceit, but in humility consider others as more important than yourselves (Philippians 2:3 HCSB).*

Insights on Introversion

What impact does this trait have on relationships?

For an Introvert, it is critical to have time to think through new information before making a group decision, even when they've been asked just to throw some ideas out there for everyone to consider. Brainstorming sessions are not where you'll get the best input from an Introvert, who usually will find them almost overwhelming. Concerning brainstorming sessions, I've often thought it would be interesting to see what would result if the Extraverts and Introverts were put into separate rooms. The Extraverts would probably go at it in their usual boisterous style, with everyone talking and contributing, and the Introverts would most likely want to write the key discussion points on a large pad or whiteboard and take about 15 to 20 minutes to think about these points before having to discuss them. It is likely that the joint brainstorming session would be more productive if this could be done.

With Introverts, new information must go into their personal 'think tank' for a while before they're comfortable with expounding on that information. It's important for Introverts to have some alone time to process their thoughts. Too many distractions can be detrimental to their thinking process.

What can Introverts do to improve their relationships?

If you're an Introvert and someone is pressing you for an answer before you're ready to give one, try not to take the silent route; ask them to give you some time to think over the matter. Then when you feel as though you've had a chance to collect your thoughts, let them know your answer. If it's something they need an immediate response to, preface your answer with something like, *"For what it's worth,* or *my immediate reaction would be* _____; however, I haven't had time to really think this over. When I get that opportunity, if I have other thoughts on the subject, I'll let you know."

Life application verse:

> *When I think on my ways, I turn my feet to your testimonies; I hasten and do not delay to keep your commandments (Psalm 119:59-60 ESV).*

6. Learning Styles of Extraverts and Introverts

- ☐ **Extraverts** figure things out best when they can talk with someone else about an issue or a problem.

☐ **Introverts** figure things out best when they have time alone to think things through.

Insights on Extraversion

What impact does this trait have on relationships?

It is important for the Extravert to have someone who will listen to them, not for psychological reasons, but because as they speak, they clarify their thoughts. Just as the Introvert needs time alone to process their thoughts, the Extravert needs interaction with others to help solidify their decision on a matter and come to the best conclusion.

Before I understood the differences between Introversion and Extraversion, Linda would begin to speak to me about an idea or thought she had, and after a couple of sentences, I would tell her that what she was saying didn't make sense. This was hurtful to her, and made her feel like something was wrong with her.

When we became aware that she was just being the Extravert God made her to be, it all made sense. This was a predisposition that related to Linda's strong *tendencies toward Extraversion*. I now encourage her to read aloud or communicate her thoughts, especially when she is trying to process new information.

What can Extraverts do to improve their relationships?

When Linda says, "I need some talk time," this means she just needs clarification on some information that she's trying to process.

Extraverts will find that discussing your need with someone for this sort of "sounding board" conversation is essential. The person whom you communicate with should give non-critical feedback to help you clarify matters and gain new understanding.

Life application verse:

A word spoken at the right time is like golden apples on a silver tray (Proverbs 25:11 HCSB).

Insights on Introversion

What impact does this trait have on relationships?

We've clarified the fact that Introverts process information internally and thus they need a lot of alone time. But life doesn't always allow us to take all the solitary time we need to make decisions. With that in mind, let's move on to the challenge of what Introverts can do to improve their relationships.

What can Introverts do to improve their relationships?

Introverts need to practice vocalizing their thoughts and ideas. They might even need to join organizations such as Toastmasters to become more proficient at public speaking. This would be a huge challenge for an Introvert, but it would pay tremendous dividends. If you're an Introvert, volunteer to give your testimony before small men's or women's groups to gain practice in speaking in front of others, or volunteer to lead small teams at work or small Bible study groups at church. If you're in a small group at church, start by asking the leader if you can lead one of the sessions. Self-consciousness melts away when you speak to the needs of the audience or impart your experience or expertise on a topic in which you're proficient.

Another way to practice reaching out to others (when your natural tendency is to be withdrawn) is to make an effort to get to know someone better, and to find out as much about them as you can without being rude. Listen to what they have to say. This will open the door of conversation between the two of you, since most people enjoy talking about themselves. Once the conversation is flowing, mutual questions and the natural give-and-take of communication will occur more easily between you. All the while you are doing these things you are growing as a person. It may not seem like it at first.

It may even seem like you're making a fool of yourself, and maybe you are at first, but don't stop trying. I will use my own experience in this area as an example of how I learned to practice Extraversion at times when my natural tendency was to be Introverted.

I have three daughters. When they were in grade school, they all brought home flyers that advertised the start of a girls' softball league. I played a lot of baseball as a child, and when my daughters expressed their eagerness to participate in the softball league, it motivated me to go to the community meeting at the local middle school.

At that meeting, the national director of the softball league organization got up and presented the outline for starting a league in our community. Toward the end of his speech, he said he needed volunteers, and the first volunteer he needed was for someone to be the president of the local chapter. With that, he took the red and white softball he had been holding and threw it right at me. Of course, my natural reaction was to catch the ball. Then he said something that made my heart sink down to my size 10 1/2 shoes.

"I decided before I began speaking that the person to catch this ball when I threw it would be the new president of the league," he quipped as he stared at me as if waiting for a response he already knew he would get. As I stood there and thought about it, I considered, *I like baseball, my daughters want to play, and after all, I'm the vice president of operations and a partner in my company whose sales are 10 million a year; this should be a piece of cake.* I accepted the position. We organized other volunteers, and soon there was a girls' softball league in our community.

The one thing I didn't consider, however, was that after getting flyers out to the community and calling for another meeting (which would fill the entire auditorium with parents and their daughters who wanted to play ball), I would take the role that the national director had taken previously: it was now my responsibility to explain how the league would operate.

On the night of the meeting, I began to get nervous. I had never done any public speaking before. I knew it was too late to back out, though, so I mustered up my courage and stood before the sea of faces looking at me eagerly, expectantly, and said, "Good evening, ladies and gentlemen …"

And then it happened: my worst fears came to pass. I had completely forgotten what I wanted to say. Fortunately, the man from the national organization was there, and when he saw the look of desperation on my face, he quickly took over as I slowly began to walk to the back of the stage. It was the most humiliating experience I've ever had in my life. Even though I wanted to resign, I hung in there and saw the project through, and we had a successful girls' softball league in our city. Yes, I did have to get up and speak many more times at awards banquets and various meetings, but I never froze up again. Thank God.

I eventually came to know Christ, a decision that prompted me to sell my business and enter full time ministry. Over the last 35 years I have spoken publicly thousands of times at a variety of venues, including weddings, funerals, special events, and during many Sunday morning and Wednesday evening services.

You may be wondering something I used to question myself about frequently: As someone who tends to be an Introvert, how and why did I go into full time ministry, especially knowing that public speaking didn't come easily for me? There are several reasons. Then as now, it was and still is my personal conviction that God called me to the ministry, so whether or not I was an expert at public speaking, I choose to follow His direction and leading in my life.

I also came to understand the truth of the phrase, "There is nothing to fear but fear itself." This is especially true when you have God on your side. I decided I would not allow fear to defeat me or set the limitations of my personal growth. In all my experiences over the years, God has seen me through many difficult situations, especially at times when my natural abilities or predispositions haven't been able to carry me. Whatever the cost, I've learned to take the challenges of life and push on. I can't say that I've come out victoriously on every occasion, but I have learned and grown from every occasion. This attitude has helped me do things I would not have considered attempting earlier in my life.

Let me return to my focus on Introversion for a moment. Those of us who are Introverts must be honest with ourselves and ask, is it my Introversion or my lack of self-confidence that holds me back? Is it Introversion, or am I struggling with a poor self-image? Am I responding negatively to statements made about me and to me by important people in my life regarding what appear to be my shortcomings? All of these elements were a big part of why I froze up at my first public speaking opportunity. The mental picture I painted of myself prior to my harrowing experience was distorted, and many influential people in my life had a hand in creating my perspective. I had believed the negative words spoken about me by others. It is important for each of us to step back and realize that whatever happened to us yesterday isn't what defines who we are today as much as how we responded or behaved in any given situation or encounter with others.

Being defined is a lifelong process. I've heard it said that life isn't like a snapshot; it's like a video: the scenery and behavior change with each frame. Take control of your life. Other people's opinions of you, especially if they have derogatory things to say to you, must remain with them. My advice is to not partner with them in their opinions. There is such a thing as constructive input about your behavior, and you should be able to learn from and receive that kind of input, but you also need to recognize when someone is simply trying to tear you down. Don't partner with them; let them own their negative behavior, and you move on with your life.

Keep in mind another truth about human nature: When someone has derogatory, hurtful things to say about you, they are speaking from their own brokenness. I'll say it again – don't partner with them. See their negativism as a red flag of caution, but also as an opportunity to minister health and wholeness to them instead of simply reacting to their behavior.

Life application verse:

*Be strong and courageous. Do not fear or be in dread of them, for it is the L*ORD *your God who goes with you. He will not leave you or forsake you (Deuteronomy 31:6 HCSB).*

CHAPTER 5

COMPARING THE TWO PERCEIVING FUNCTIONS: SENSING AND INTUITION

As we gather information throughout the course of our lives, we use the perception functions of Sensing and Intuition. However, these functions are opposites; thus, we can't use both at once, and we're unable to use both functions equally well. As you determine your personality type, you'll discover that you tend to use one or the other predominantly. You will prefer either Sensing or Intuition as your primary way of gathering data.

I have learned the importance and value of understanding both of these perceiving functions. As I mentioned earlier, I prefer Sensing as my primary way to gather information. Because most Sensors see everything in black and white they tend to limit their creativity. However, Sensors excel in seeing and doing things in a consistent manner and making improvements to the practical applications of already existing systems and processes. These are the natural attributes of the Sensor.

Intuitives, on the other hand, see no limits to their potential, and as a result, they can be very creative in approaching life.

There are positive and negative aspects of both Sensing and Intuition, which we will cover as we compare these opposite functions of perception. However, as a Sensor and a Christian, it was a huge revelation to me when I realized the value of developing

Intuitive perception. Anyone who exercises faith exercises it through the perceptive function of Intuition.

> *"Now faith is the substance of things hoped for, the evidence of things not seen." (Hebrews 11:1 NKJV)*

If Sensors can grasp this truth it has the potential to take them to a new level in their faith. You cannot exercise faith through Sensing, because according to Scripture, it is impossible to do so.

Faith is not looking at the facts or the tangible or the black and white of what we Sensors consider reality. Whatever is already tangible requires no faith. Faith is always looking with hope toward a future manifestation of something that is *not seen*, whether it relates to a promise from the Bible or the second coming of Christ. In essence, faith is initiated through the function of Intuition, *not* through the function of Sensing. This truth revolutionized my Christian walk. Suddenly I discovered that if I developed my Intuitive function, I would also increase my ability to grow in faith.

So how did I go about doing this?

I think all Christians understand it is essential to read the Bible, memorize verses and bone up on historical facts in order to enhance their understanding of the Bible and relationship with God. I have done that from the time I became a Christian. But if we want to have the Bible impact on us at a personal level where it becomes God's Word to us we must learn to let it speak to us in a personal way. When Jesus would use the phrase *"he who has ears to hear"*, He was not talking about our physical hearing system. He was talking about the ability we have to hear that inner voice. That characteristic in humans is their Intuitive capability. My challenge to you is to consciously read the Bible for revelation and not just for filling your head with dates, facts, and bits of Bible information. This passage from Hebrews is clear about reading the Bible for revelation:

> *For the word of God is living and effective and sharper than any two-edged sword, penetrating as far as to divide soul, spirit, joints, and marrow; it is a judge of the ideas and thoughts of the heart (Hebrews 4:12 HCSB).*

Obviously, the power of God's Word to *divide soul, spirit, joints, and marrow,* and to *judge the ideas and thoughts of the heart*, goes beyond the level of reading the Bible for the sake of acquiring information. It requires what I call devotional reading. This involves allowing the living Word of God to fill our hearts and spirits, giving us personal revelation about our life and lifestyle. The transforming power of the Word, combined with the voice of the Holy Spirit is available to us through the conduit of Intuition. It relates to God speaking to us personally.

On the other hand, if your natural preference is to use your Intuitive function, it is extremely important for you to verify what you believe you are hearing through your internal hearing system by the written Word of God. All personal revelation needs to line up with the written Word of God, maybe not with chapter and verse but surly in principle.

My approach to personal relationships changed dramatically when I understood these tendencies of mine, which are inherent for most Sensors. My ability to impart grace in my relationships with others has increased tenfold, thus also giving me the ability to reach out to someone who is struggling in their faith. My focus is not so much on someone's current inappropriate behavior but on the unseen events and brokenness in their life that has brought them to the decisions they are making currently.

Before moving on to the section where we'll examine the opposite aspects of Sensing and Intuition, let me make an important observation. During our years of teaching at the Introduction to Biblical Counseling Schools at Youth With A Mission bases around the world, a standard question has always been asked. Before I tell you the question, keep in mind we have been teaching these classes three times a year for twenty-two years, with each class averaging about thirty-five students with about fourteen different nations represented.

The question I'm always asked is, "Which personality type should I marry?"

My standard answer is, "A born-again Christian with similar spiritual goals as you." The spiritual compatibility factors are always the most important criteria for choosing a life partner. Marrying someone based on personality traits alone can get you in big trouble. But, understanding their personality traits will go a long way toward growing a harmonious marriage.

The Sensing and Intuitive functions are, in my opinion, the most important of all the functions to understand. This is because all communication is based on our perceptions, and if we start a conversation by making judgments, as some personality types do, then we must remember that those judgments are based on our perceptions, which can be flawed. Linda and I are both Sensors; *therefore,* we start the communication process from a reality-based standpoint, talking about things we know to be true based on information we've gathered with our five senses. This makes it easier to clarify the topic being discussed, and it keeps us on "the same page of music" as opposed to discussing things that are perceived intuitively, which can be anything in the gray area of the issue.

We have counseled many married couples over the years; thus, we've worked with couples where both spouses are Intuitive, or more difficult yet, couples where the spouses are opposites, meaning one is a Sensor and the other is an Intuitive. When couples are experiencing difficulty in the communication process, we talk to them about the importance of having a clear starting point for both parties as they begin their conversations, and particularly as they discuss any important issue. Many misunderstandings and frustrations can be avoided when couples understand the different dynamics involved in the two functions of perception, Sensing and Intuition. In counseling, this understanding has helped many couples make great improvements in their communication.

1. How Sensors and Intuitives Perceive the World around Them

- ☐ **Sensors** perceive the world around them by gathering information about tangible things through sensory input: whatever they can see, smell, hear, feel, and taste.

☐ **Intuitives** attempt to find meaning in what they perceive, and to identify possibilities and relationships. That which *might be possible* is always on the mind of the Intuitive.

Insights on Sensing

What impact does this trait have on relationships?

A Sensor is very good at seeing all of the details. Sensors are often found in vocations such as engineering, law enforcement and the military to name a few. Any vocation requiring Sensing Perception would be good for the Sensors. Some of the greatest chefs in the world are those whose dominant function is Sensing, as they use their keen sense of taste to produce their creations.

Sensors live in the here and now; they do not project into the future very well, nor are they good at being the original creator of something. This doesn't mean they can't improve on someone else's original creation because they can improve on that which has been an Intuitive's original idea. This is true for me as a Sensor. When a situation requires seeing something that doesn't exist or even forecasting, I find it difficult to do either of those things. In these situations, I ask my Intuitive friends for some input.

What can Sensors do to improve their relationships?

Sensors need to understand that there is more to the situation than meets the eye. Sensors also need to learn not to throw cold water on the ideas and solutions of their Intuitive friends or they may not remain friends very long.

Life application verse:

By faith we understand that the universe was created by the word of God, so that what is seen has been made from things that are not visible (Hebrews 11:3 HCSB).

Insights on Intuition

What impact does this trait have on relationships?

The Intuitive is motivated to overcome obstacles that get in the way of anything they're trying to accomplish. They can be so intrigued by possibilities or connections they become carried away with the challenge. That can be good or bad, depending on the results. Some of our greatest inventors spent most of their lives working on things that didn't seem possible to those around them. Because of their creative nature and the many ideas they have, Intuitives quite often aren't taken very seriously by their friends, who typically accuse them of having their head in the clouds. This is frustrating to the Intuitive, who will endeavor to prove that their ideas have validity.

What can Intuitives do to improve their relationships?

For the Intuitive, it's important to understand that 76% of the population perceives things with their Sensing function, and thus they do not see many of the intangibles that Intuitives see on a regular basis. If you're an Intuitive, hopefully this explanation brings some comfort to you and helps you understand why so many people don't seem to understand where you're coming from with your perceptions. This should relieve some of your frustration and make you more at ease in your relationships with others, especially when you're interacting with people who prefer the Sensing function.

Life application verse:

Therefore, preparing your minds for action, and being sober-minded, set your hope fully on the grace that will be brought to you at the revelation of Jesus Christ. (1 Peter 1:13 NKJV)

2. Limitations and Possibilities for both Sensors and Intuitives

- ☐ **Sensors** live in the real world and see what exists, not what they wish could exist. They are realists: they see all of the limits of any given situation.

- ☐ **Intuitives** prefer the world of imagination where their potential seems limitless. They are excited by the thought of what *could* be possible if all barriers were removed.

Insights on Sensing

What impact does this trait have on relationships?

Sensors have the ability to see why an idea, a plan, or a proposed solution to a problem simply will not work. That is an ability, especially when applied to a problem that needs solving, but it is also a weakness, because Sensors tend to limit their own lives because of this trait. Their realism keeps them from accomplishing some things that would be possible with a little creativity. Seeing the limitations can appear to be a very negative approach to life: i.e., the "glass being half empty" approach. There was a time that my *Intuitive* friends learned to keep their ideas to themselves when they were around me because I'm capable of telling them all the reasons why their ideas won't work. That's frustrating to an Intuitive, and I used to wonder why my friends didn't talk to me much anymore.

What can Sensors do to improve their relationships?

I have learned to listen to the ideas of my Intuitive friends even when I don't quite see how their ideas can be successful based on what they've told me. I don't discourage them. If I see a detail they've missed, I will express it as an observation type question: *"Great idea, but I'm curious: how are you going to provide for …"* When a question is framed in this manner, it helps get their creative juices flowing again. It also points them in the direction towards what they need to do to fill in the gaps of their expansive ideas. Sometimes I do them a big favor because I point out something that would actually keep their idea from working. But it's important to let an Intuitive discover for themselves that an idea or plan will or will not work instead of just telling them. When it comes to creating, Sensors and Intuitives make a great team as long as they work together to understand their different strengths and weaknesses.

Life application verse:

> *Let no corrupt word proceed out of your mouth, but what is good for necessary edification, that it may impart grace to the hearers (Ephesians 4:29 NKJV).*

Insights on Intuition

The Intuitive loves the world of imagination. I think Walt Disney was one of the most successful Intuitives this world has ever known. Using the medium of animation, he created anything and everything he conjured up with his incredible imagination. In the world of imagination, there are no failures. However, in the real world, there are "laws of design" that are absolute.

If you're an Intuitive, I know that this statement just challenges you to prove me wrong. I also know there is a law of diminishing returns. The *Intuitives* tendency is to believe if you look at every conceivable angle of a concept or relationship issue long enough, you will eventually figure out a way to get it to work. Many times this is true, and we have a new invention as a result, but the question the *Intuitive* must ask is, at what cost?

What can Intuitives do to improve their relationships?

The Intuitive must be diligent in determining (and then acknowledging) what is real and what is not. We live in a world that requires us to pay attention to the details, and sometimes this seems to be the Intuitives Achilles heel. Intuitives also need to place some limits on how much time they spend in their imaginary world and learn to stay on task with the day-to-day routine's that have to get done. Intuitives can also practice listening to their Sensing friends when they express concerns about some of the Intuitives ideas. This could keep the Intuitive from getting lost in trying to solve some unsolvable issues.

Life application verse:

> *For which of you, wanting to build a tower, doesn't first sit down and calculate the cost to see if he has enough to complete it? (Luke 14:28 HCSB)*

3. Learning Styles of Sensors and Intuitives

- ☐ **Sensors** see things sequentially. They grasp the details, but find it hard to see the big picture.

- ☐ **Intuitives** see conceptually: they have an easy time seeing the big picture, but have difficulty with the details.

Insights on Sensing

What impact does this trait have on relationships?

Sensors and Intuitives have a different experience in the educational process. Sensors are more comfortable with the teaching methods used by teachers in grade school, middle school, and high school than with the methods used by college professors. In the lower grade levels, the tendency is to teach subjects sequentially through memorization and redundancy. This is perfect for the way Sensors learn. The higher in the educational process, the more difficult it becomes to grasp and retain concepts, because the tendency in higher education is to include concepts and theory in the teaching process. To Sensors there are too many gray areas, and it becomes more difficult to fill in the gaps, so to speak, that a lot of instruction in theory leaves open. Sensors find the overall challenge to be difficult, but there's no question that college courses help Sensors develop Intuitive skills.

What can Sensors do to improve their relationships?

Sensors shouldn't take the path of least resistance when it comes to theory and concepts. What I mean by that is allow some time for creativity and imagination to work in your life. You can purpose to do so by reading about "creative thinking" or take a class on "creative writing". Asking God in your prayer times to give you vision concerning your future is essential both to living a God directed life and expanding your Intuitive capabilities. I do all of the above and it has helped me put a higher value on my own imagination and creativity. The result is you become more creative and spiritually sensitive.

Life application verse:

> Oh, taste and see that the LORD is good! Blessed is the man who takes refuge in him! (Psalm 34:8 NKJV)

Insights on Intuition

What impact does this trait have on relationships?

Regarding the education process, my Intuitive friends tell me they were bored with the methods used in the lower grade levels, and some of them even got in trouble for acting up in class. However, they began to excel as they progressed to higher grade levels and on into college because they were required to make Intuitive connections in the subject matter. Intuitive Thinkers excel in technical careers, research and development, medicine, psychiatry, and law. If someone is Intuitive and a Feeler, he or she will excel in vocations that are oriented toward helping people, such as counseling of any kind, teaching, social services, missions work, volunteerism, and so on.

What can Intuitives do to improve their relationships?

For the Intuitive, it's important to become immersed in the details of the big picture or the concept to examine it for missing links. If you're an Intuitive, whatever you can do to get involved in the detailed aspect of processes will help. Another great way is to commit to read through the Bible in a year, (Including all of the genealogies) and look for things you've never seen before. Not only will you improve in your Bible knowledge but you will also improve your ability to use your Sensing function. Another good way to become sharper with your Sensing function is to balance your checkbook manually and not with a computer program, or keep up with statistics regarding whatever vocation you may be involved in.

The point is that if you don't use the opposing perceiving function you will not develop it. It's like being right handed and tying you left hand behind you back.

Life application verse:

> *He was with God in the beginning. All things were created through Him, and apart from Him not one thing was created that has been created (John 1:2 HCSB).*

4. The Different Communication Styles of Sensors and Intuitives

- □ **Sensors** are specific and literal when speaking, writing, or listening. They describe the facts first, and may or may not get to the general point.

- □ **Intuitives** are more general and abstract in their speaking, writing, or listening. They may make a general point without describing the facts.

Insights on Sensing

What impact does this trait have on relationships?

If an Intuitive comes to me with a concept or an idea and they don't give me an opportunity to ask for more details, I will be lost. As a Sensor I build the big picture the same way a puzzle is completed: one piece at a time. In times past when communicating with an Intuitive, I've thought, *I must really be stupid* or, *They sure are marching to a different drumbeat* or, *I can't get there from here*. None of these statements is accurate. When I am communicating with anyone the first bit of information I need is, what perceiving function do they use? This is more difficult in a new relationship than with someone you've known for a while but if you listen closely you can tell whether they are Intuitive or Sensing.

Let me share another example from my life. I served on staff at a large church as the executive Pastor. Every year we would use our annual church birthday as a way to celebrate the ministry of the church but more than that as an outreach to the community. As we grew the church celebrations became more and more elaborate. I was in charge of organizing these events. The senior pastor was an ENTP. We actually worked very well together. My ESTJ administrative skills were very helpful in putting feet to the many ideas our ENTP pastor came up with.

This particular year my pastor called me into his office to discuss the celebration. He didn't give a lot of detail, which in many cases is the way of the Intuitive perceiver. All he told me was that he wanted to do the celebration at the Los Angeles County Fairgrounds. He asked that I contact them and set up an appointment to see what they have available. I made the arrangements and because I have been to the fairgrounds on many occasions I asked if we could see a particular building that was their smallest building and at the same time much larger than we had ever needed before.

When we arrived at the fairgrounds the fairground representative took us to the building I asked to see. We walked into the huge building and my pastor said "do you have anything larger"? The representative said, yes we do and took us to a building about twice the size. I thought to myself, you could play football inside this building! At that point my pastor said, "do you have anything larger"? My mouth dropped as the representative said yes, and we continued on to the largest building at the LA County Fairgrounds. We entered into the center of the building and to give you and idea of it's size, it was one football field wide and three football fields long and a huge water fountain was in the middle of the building. My pastor said, "this is perfect!" Since I knew I would be organizing this event I went numb. Then my pastor began to unveil his vision for the actual celebration.

As I listened to him come up with one creative idea after another I realized that the detail of his vision was taking place on the spot. He filled the building with events and activities through his Intuitive perceptive function as we walked around the perimeter of the inside of the building. I was taking notes as fast as I could. I knew he would leave the details to me.

Without sharing all of those details the event came off beautifully, even gaining the accolades of the fair ground representative as one of the best events they had seen in that facility.

What can Sensors do to improve their relationships?

A Sensor needs to identify whether they are interacting with another Sensor or an Intuitive. Once that is accomplished, the Sensor can determine the best way to communicate to bring the most clarity to the conversation. If you're a Sensor, try to look at things conceptually without feeling compelled to have all the details first before "buying in" to an idea or plan. Conversely, when you as a Sensor present an idea to an Intuitive, be careful not to put them to sleep with loads of unimportant details. As a Sensor, I've learned to get my thoughts and ideas reduced to a broad sweeping paragraph and then let Intuitives ask the questions they want to ask, which are usually very few.

Life application verse:

As they heard these things, he proceeded to tell a parable, because he was near to Jerusalem, and because they supposed that the kingdom of God was to appear immediately (Luke 19:11 HCSB).

Insights on Intuition

What impact does this trait have on relationships?

I have a close friend that is an ENFP and she has told me:
"I feel like I am misunderstood much of the time, whether I'm communicating with a Sensor or another Intuitive. I find myself pausing and re-explaining in different ways to make my ideas understandable to others. I don't mind doing this but sometimes it does get frustrating".

Back to the story about the annual church celebration. At the point my pastor asked me to make arrangements at the LA County Fairgrounds, he knew that was all he needed to tell me and I would do it no questions asked. We had learned how to flow together because we had worked together for five prior years. In the beginning of our relationship it took a while for us to understand one another. It was trial and error much of the time. He came to realize that in order for me to understand his concepts and ideas he needed to give more detail than he was comfortable with. Frankly, it was because he didn't have the detail yet just the concept. But he did his best to get his idea across. He allowed me to ask a lot of questions, some of which he would simply say, "I don't know yet" and I could live with that. The key for us was that we didn't get frustrated and give up on each other.

What can Intuitives do to improve their relationships?

When an Intuitive is interacting with a Sensor, the Intuitive needs to help the Sensor understand whatever concept or theory they're discussing by giving more details than they would usually prefer to give. The Intuitive has to be careful not to oversimplify, because they might get a response like, "Yes, I'm not stupid! I'm following what you're saying!" If you're an Intuitive and you recognize yourself in this description, keep in mind that the difference between you and a Sensor is not an intelligence issue; it's a perception issue. You see the big picture, and the Sensor focuses on the details within that big picture. Both are important.

Life application verse:

> *Remind them of these things, and charge them before God not to quarrel about words, which does no good, but only ruins the hearers (2 Timothy 2:14 ESV).*

5. Problems that Sensors and Intuitives Are Best at Solving

- ☐ **Sensors** are quick to see solutions to practical, concrete problems.

- ☐ **Intuitives** often come up with imaginative solutions to complex or theoretical problems.

Insights on Sensing

What impact does this trait have on relationships?

Most Sensors quickly admit that they're not best suited to repair glitches in computer programs or even detecting the problem with a computer that doesn't work. On the other hand, they do a fine job of making repairs on computers themselves once the theoretical problems are sifted through and the real problem is discovered. If it's a mechanical system, Sensors can usually go through a process of elimination to find the problem and fix it. Even if it's a relational issue, once they know enough about the situation they can usually see where the breakdowns are in the relationship and help people get things ironed out.

What can Sensors do to improve their relationships?

Be honest with others and themselves about what is easy for them to accomplish and what is difficult for them. As mentioned earlier a Sensor is good at creating improvements on what has already been established. On the other hand, if a Sensor needs to come up with a creative solution to alleviate a problem, they will probably end up frustrated. Call on your Intuitive friends and associates to get some fresh insight. They can help.

Life application verse:

> a wise man will listen and increase his learning, and a discerning man will obtain guidance (Proverbs 1:5 HCSB).

Insights on Intuition

What impact does this trait have on relationships?

Both Intuitive Thinkers and Intuitive Feelers love the challenge of solving problems that require creativity. The NT tends to be more technical. One time a young couple we know invited Linda and me over for dinner. The husband was an ENTP, one very creative individual. He proceeded to show me an elaborate gadget he invented that would make iced tea when he pulled a string from the chair he sat in on the other side of the room. Please don't expect me to explain it to you. He was obviously going through a period of boredom in his life. One of the downsides to all of that creativity every NT should take seriously is that they can get so caught up in their problem solving and creativity they don't have time to develop their relationship skills. This can cause some major problems along the way.

Intuitive Feelers get so caught up in helping people solve their relationship problems they neglect other priorities in their lives. Most of the time, those other priorities have to do with things that seem trivial to them, like paying their bills on time or putting gas in the car! Enough said here, I think most Intuitive Feelers can tell stories about missing some of the important details in their lives.

What can Intuitives do to improve their relationships?

The downfall of an Intuitive Thinker is that they're always trying to build a better mousetrap when the old one works fine; likewise, Intuitive Feelers tend to "help" someone when they don't want help. The Intuitive needs to be careful not to obsess over problem solving. As I mentioned previously, the law of diminishing returns comes into play with personality attributes that seem like strengths: remember, a strength push to an extreme becomes a weakness. The Intuitive needs to become better at recognizing when that line has been crossed.

Life application verse:

> *Look carefully then how you walk, not as unwise but as wise, making the best use of the time, because the days are evil. Therefore do not be foolish, but understand what the will of the Lord is (Ephesians 5:15 HCSB).*

6. How Sensors and Intuitives Prefer to Work

- ☐ **Sensors** focus on the necessary specifics to carry out an assignment. They are very detail-oriented.

- ☐ **Intuitives** are comfortable with theory and abstractions. They like developing new concepts.

Insights on Sensing

What impact does this trait have on relationships?

A Sensor's motto is "Bring on the Standard Operating Procedures." Most Sensors appreciate things like SOPs or detailed job descriptions. Some Sensors like hands-on training, but most of them just want to go to work and get things produced or finished. I am a classic Sensor. When I'm in a situation where I don't have the specifics to carry out an assignment, I will usually write my own job description or procedures as I figure out what is required to get the job done. Sensors relate to their world by what they do and how well they do it. Later when we look at Temperament Core Needs you will see that for the SJ Temperament they desire to have relationships with people and institutions but they want to earn their way into that relationship by living up to and exceeding any expectations people and institutions place on them.

What can Sensors do to improve their relationships?

Vocationally or relationally, Sensors need to understand what is being asked of them before they accept a new job assignment or role. Sensors should try and pin down the person that will have expectations on them and get a full understanding of those expectations. Life becomes less stressful for you when you know what is expected. Otherwise you will experience various levels of stress until you figure out what you are supposed to be doing.

Life application verse:

> *And God is able to provide you with every blessing in abundance, so that having all contentment in all things at all times, you may abound in every good work (2 Corinthians 9:8).*

Insights on Intuition

What impact does this trait have on relationships?

Intuitives dislike being constrained by a detailed job description and a list of standard operating procedures. Their preference is to have the freedom to develop an environment where they can use their creativity. Unlike Sensors and their need for job descriptions and procedures, the Intuitive needs only a general idea of what the desired goal is and they will take it from there. The finished product may or may not look like what was expected by someone else, but the Intuitive will like it. Best vocations for the Intuitive are those that allow for a lot of leeway and creativity on the part of the intuitive.

What can Intuitives do to improve their relationships?

In your job, don't be afraid to express yourself concerning your need to use your creativity on a daily basis. If your job requires a lot of routine and redundancy, do yourself and your boss a favor and begin to search for a job that requires what you have to offer as a creative, concept-oriented, big-picture Intuitive. Things won't get better for either of you by just trying to grind it out. If you're in the wrong job, begin to look for the right job. The sooner you come to that decision (that your current job is a bad fit for you), the better off you'll be. Also, when working on a project with your Sensor coworkers, remind them that you will approach the project differently than they might, so that when you do, they will lighten up and not get frustrated by expecting you to tackle the project with a detail-oriented approach.

Life application verse:

> *But Martha was distracted with much serving. And she went up to him and said, "Lord, do you not care that my sister has left me to serve alone? Tell her then to help me." But the Lord answered her, "Martha, Martha, you are anxious and troubled about many things, but one thing is necessary. Mary has chosen the good portion, which will not be taken away from her" (Luke 10:40).*

CHAPTER 6

ISSUES THAT IMPACT THE TWO JUDGING FUNCTIONS: THINKING AND FEELING

I want to elaborate a bit on the Judging functions of Thinking and Feeling before we look at the individual characteristics of each. As we get into more detail, it won't take long before you recognize elements that could be attributed to males or females. Statistics tell us that 70% of the male population and 30% of the female population in the United States uses Thinking as their primary judging function. Of course, the gender percentages are the reverse for the function of Feeling. When I made this discovery years ago, my thoughts went to the many books that had been written about male and female differences. Most books in that genre tend to categorize all women the same and all men the same, thus completely ignoring the fact that 30% of men have a trait that is predominant in women (the Feeling function), and 30 % of women have a trait that is predominant in men (the Thinking function).

In the seminars we've done over the years, this revelation has made the biggest impact on those women and men. As a society, we expect all men to approach decision making in a logical, analytical manner, and all women to make decisions based on their personal values. Men and women who are in that 30% minority have struggled throughout life with the expectations leveled on them by family, friends, and society in general. Linda and I have spent many hours in counseling with both men and women who have felt like a square peg being forced into a round hole for most of their lives. When the light goes on and they realize that God created them with the unique predisposition for decision-making they have, they experience tremendous relief, and almost immediately, their confusion dissipates.

Your Emotions and the Function of Feeling

When the word Feeling is used in Myers-Briggs terminology to describe a judging function, it does not mean the same thing as your emotions. The Feeling function is a rational method people use to come to conclusions about information they have gathered. There is a connection with a Feeler's emotions because the emotions give input regarding personal values. When you give preference to the Feeling function and you make a decision about anything that is important to you, your emotions will get involved in the process. However, you are not doing the *evaluating* with your emotions. Your emotions give additional insight that will have an impact on your Feeling evaluations. Generally, a person who prefers Feeling as their way to come to conclusions interacts with their emotions regularly and with a relative amount of ease. In a sense, if you prefer the Feeling function for decision-making, you have an additional filter, as the information is tested emotionally.

Your Emotions and the Function of Thinking

The Thinking function is a rational process just as the Feeling function is. However, those who prefer the Thinking function put their trust in logic, analysis of cause and effect, and truth and principles. The Thinking function will not naturally allow emotions to give input. Emotions rarely line up with logic and principles. This does not mean that a person who prefers the Thinking function is not an emotional being. On the contrary, they have very strong emotions that they know will impact their behavior. Sometimes Thinkers do have moments that include emotional reactions. They also have deep personal values. When a Thinker's emotions rise up over a threatened value, the Thinker will react emotionally, but usually they don't like the experience. The Thinker prefers to stay cool-headed and approach all decisions through the standard Thinker's method: analysis of the situation

Other Elements that Impact Our Judging Functions

Each of us has a philosophy of life that we've developed over the years, and it is as unique as our personality. We are continually tweaking what we believe to be true and false, valuable or of no value.

There are many things that impact our belief system. The following are some of what I consider the major elements: our inborn predisposition for either the Thinking or Feeling function; our personality characteristics; our culture; our age and the season of life we're in at any given time; our education; our vocation; and our friends. On the spiritual side of things, we are shaped by our childhood religious upbringing, by our current faith, and by whether or not we believe in input from spiritual powers of darkness or from the Holy Spirit. Together, these elements form our belief system, both consciously and subconsciously.

To simplify matters, I will place these elements in three broad categories:

1) Inborn personality preferences and the core needs of our temperament

2) Life Experiences, childhood experiences and upbringing, family, education, and our vocation

3) Spiritual experiences, both positive and negative; God's revealed purpose for our life; His Word and the Holy Spirit

These three categories form our *expectations*, which are the driving force behind most of our actions. We have conscious and subconscious expectations of others and ourselves. Our expectations must be evaluated each time we are disappointed in our own actions or the actions or outcome of any given event or relationship crisis. If we look honestly and deeply enough at most of our conflicts in life, what we'll find at the heart of the disagreement or disappointment is a conflict between our own expectations and the expectations of others about the situation. Many, if not most of our expectations are not known to the person or organization on whom we place the expectation. Linda and I have found this to be true in the marriage counseling we have done over the years. Expectations are really the "**rules**" we have about life and relationships. Some of the rules are made known and some are not, even to ourselves. When the rules are broken, we respond with anger, fear, disappointment, judgment, and so on, because we've come to a conclusion about the results prior to an encounter with someone or a difficult situation in an organization of which we're a part. When they fail to live up to our expectations (our unwritten "rules"), the value we place on the person or organization begins to diminish in our mind until eventually, we want nothing to do with them. All the while, our expectations (which can sometimes be false) are the determining factor in the conclusions we draw.

With this in mind, I want to look at a scriptural parallel to this statement. The apostle Paul in first Corinthians was writing about the Corinthians' incorrect approach to a relationship with God. He makes an incredible statement in verse six:

He has made us competent to be ministers of a new covenant, not of the letter, but of the Spirit; for the letter kills, but the Spirit produces life (2 Corinthians 3:6).

Paul was emphasizing a principle that was essential for the Corinthians' understanding of what would not work in trying to please God: *"The letter kills and the Spirit produces life."* My paraphrase of this verse would be, 'You'll die trying to please God with your actions, but spiritual rebirth will bring you into relationship with Him'.

I think most believers in Christ understand this verse conceptually; however, I don't think most believers have *applied* it to their own expectations. Let me explain. Our expectations, if unmovable, are the same thing as the Law to us. If we hold tight to our expectations – our personal Law – concerning a person or an organization, they will eventually die in our eyes under the weight of our expectations. We write the Law in our relationships. Whether it is God's Law or our Law, the weight of the Law alone will kill relationships.

The ramifications of this truth are enormous. An example would be if I expect Linda to have dinner on the table every night when I get home from the office at precisely 5:00 PM, and she doesn't. I'm then disappointed in her and her value goes down in my eyes. If she continues with this behavior, I become more and more disillusioned with our relationship. If I add to that all of the other areas where she falls short of the Law, more than likely divorce will be inevitable. Of course, the example could easily go the other direction and does. I know this is an extreme example, but you can apply it to any relationship.

We become disenfranchised with one another based on how we handle our expectations. Please don't misunderstand me. I'm not promoting having no expectations in our relationships. It is important to look to the future with great expectations; that's faith. It's important to expect people and organizations to keep their word. I expect people to treat me with a certain level of respect, if for no other reason than because I am a human being created in the image of God. These are all good expectations. The problem arises when someone doesn't keep their word, or treats me like I'm worthless. Do I just find a way to disassociate with them? If that were God's approach toward us, we would all be in trouble. No, there is a better way.

I have an acrostic that has helped me keep things in proper perspective. Let's separate the word 'RELATE' into two parts: REL-ATE.

The first half of the word tells us how we should respond to the **performance** of others:

> Release
>
> Expectation
>
> Levels

The second half of the word tells us how we should respond to the **personality traits** of others:

> Appreciate (Accept)
>
> The
>
> Extremes

Let's look at the first acrostic, which relates to the performance of others. The first word "Release" indicates that we must loosen our grip on any expectations we have of others. The person or organization may be incapable in the first place, or we may be premature in having a particular expectation of their performance. When someone continues to fail in a relationship, we might even let go of all expectations so that we can be proactive in trying to minister life to that person. For example, if your child has gotten off track and become addicted to drugs or alcohol, do you write them off as a complete failure? God's way would be to make a choice to *love* them unconditionally. I'm not saying trust them unconditionally. There is a big difference between the two. Initially, I issue a certain amount of trust in my relationships with others. If trust is broken at some level, then I make adjustments regarding what a person can be trusted with in the future. If someone breaks a confidence, I won't speak to that person in confidence again. That doesn't mean I don't trust them with anything. The word "Expectations" in the acrostic has to do with your mindset toward a person or organization going into the interaction with them. Expectations can be released completely when you are in relationship with a person who operates out of their brokenness.

The third word "Levels" is just that. When someone I'm in relationship with doesn't live up to my expectations, I change the level of my expectation instead of lowering the value of the person that disappointed me (which is often our natural tendency). I think God calls this grace, and sometimes it is His mercy.

In all of this, we must keep in mind that just because we have expectations doesn't make the expectation right. Some of our expectations need to be abandoned completely. My previously held expectations for Linda to face life the same way I did was terribly wrong, and those expectations needed to be changed completely. Our marriage was deteriorating because of the expectations I was putting on her.

This second part of the acrostic relates to the personality traits of others. The first word, "Appreciate," indicates the importance of how we look at others; specifically, we must understand that God has created each of us uniquely. I think of God's creation as a mosaic: His beautiful work of art that requires all of the parts to be complete. The apostle Paul had insight into this when he described the body of Christ in First Corinthians:

So the body is not one part but many (1 Corinthians 12:14).

After we bridge "Appreciate" with the word "The," we get to the last word in the acrostic, "Extremes." This word has to do with relating to those people who are your mirror opposites and everything in between. An example would be comparing my approach to life as an ESTJ to someone who approaches life as an INFP. Without a doubt, this personality type is the hardest for me to understand, and conversely, my approach to life will at times be baffling to this person. We are different in each of the four approaches.

We all have differences, and no one is better than the other. I have come to appreciate the strengths of those who approach life differently. I believe this is exactly what God intended, and the sooner we change our perception, the better off we are. This is especially true in marriage where we are in such a long term, intimate relationship. Peter describes this well:

> *In the same way you married men should live considerately with [your wives], with an intelligent recognition [of the marriage relation] (1 Peter 3:7 The Amplified Bible).*

If we're to live considerately with each other, then we're to be considerate of our spouse's gifts, even though they are different from our own. We also shouldn't overlook the second half of the verse, *"intelligent recognition of the marriage relation,"* which has to do with evaluating why things are working or not.

It's been said, we fear that which we don't understand. I believe this is true when it comes to the differences we recognize in people's approach to life. I'm not speaking of political or religious views; I'm referring to personality traits. We need to keep in mind that personality traits are amoral. They're neither good nor bad – they're just different. I relate our personality traits to the tools we've been given by God to function on this planet. A person makes decisions using their judging functions of Thinking or Feeling, and those functions have to do with the *way* we evaluate information, not *why* we make the decisions we make.

Keep the acrostic RELATE in mind as you interact with people and organizations, and your relationships will proceed with much more harmony than they have in the past. This approach is also much more realistic than depending on your preconceived expectations, because it values the each person's unique and fascinating differences.

CHAPTER 7

Comparing the Two Judging Functions: Thinking and Feeling

We'll now look at the decision-making processes that are unique to Thinkers and Feelers, but before we go much further, let me state that we all do both. However, we can't do both simultaneously, and we don't do both equally well (or easily for that matter). Each person has a tendency toward being a Thinker or a Feeler.

1. How Thinkers and Feelers Make Decisions

- ☐ **Thinkers** look for principles to guide them in making decisions. Being logical is one of their strongest traits.

- ☐ **Feelers** sort out the values involved in the situation, meaning, determining what's important to others as well as themselves.

Insights on Thinking

What impact does this trait have on relationships?

My natural decision-making process is Thinking. Sometimes it's a double-edged sword. I have to be careful not to use only the Thinking function in every decision I make. I've learned that my reasons for making a decision are much different from my wife's reasons. Linda prefers the Feeling function and evaluates problems and situations very differently than I do. For example, in the past whenever we have looked into buying a home, I've always had my want list and she has had hers, and the two lists look very different. Mine would consist of things such as whether the purchase price would fit into our budget, the condition of the structure, what it would take to maintain the home, and what the necessary upgrades would cost. On the other hand, Linda is interested in things such as whether the kitchen is well equipped and large enough to feed the kids and grandkids; the necessity of having a guest room for family and friends to use when they come to see us; and having a dining room large enough to have family gatherings for holidays.

The evaluation processes of Thinkers and Feelers are equally valid; neither is right or wrong – they're just different. When couples understand this and learn how to make the necessary compromises, the quality of their marriage relationship improves. The same thing is true in all of our relationships. Linda and I have learned to bring healthy and fair compromises to issues that we don't readily agree on.

What can Thinkers do to improve their relationships?

As a Thinker, I always try to get input from my wife or others who use the Feeling function to come to conclusions. I have learned that my decisions lean toward justice, whereas Linda's lean more toward mercy. There is a place for both in every relationship, and in each situation we face in life. When we are counseling a couple, chances are we are dealing with a Thinker and a Feeler, so it's important to show the validity in both ways of evaluating.

Another practice for the Thinker to implement when making an important decision is a personal values check, meaning, how well the decision will mesh with their own values. This is because a Thinker's tendency is to overlook his or her values and cling to the facts when making a decision.

Life application verse:

> *Woe to you, scribes and Pharisees, hypocrites! You pay a tenth of mint, dill, and cumin, yet you have neglected the more important matters of the law – justice, mercy, and faith. These things should have been done without neglecting the others (Matthew 23:23 HCSB).*

Insights on Feeling

What impact does this trait have on relationships?

Being in a relationship with a Feeler means having someone who is caring and understanding, and who has a sincere interest in you. These are some of the strong attributes of a Feeler. The Feeler is usually easy to get to know. About the only time a relationship with the Feeler gets tense is when you ask them to violate one of their personal values. A value may be to protect their child from pain at all costs. This is not an unusual value for a Feeler.

The nature of the Feeler is to show mercy rather than seek justice. There is a delicate balance between the two. The problem is that mercy at the wrong time is not really mercy, it is enablement, that is, license to do something, which could inadvertently encourage wrongdoing. On the other hand, justice at the wrong time is abuse. When it comes to disciplining their child for something they've done wrong, something that requires discipline, the Feeler's natural tendency is to protect the child from pain. But discipline is an important part of life's learning process. The scripture is clear regarding the value of discipline.

The rod and reproof give wisdom, but a child left to himself brings shame to his mother. Discipline your son, and he will give you rest; he will give delight to your heart (Proverbs 29:15 and 17 HCSB).

A side note on parenting seems appropriate here. When raising your children, it's important to identify the difference between intentional rebellion and testing. It is natural for a child to try to discover boundaries, to see what they can get away with and what they can't. We do them a disservice if we don't help them with those discoveries. If a child is testing the boundaries, there has to be a definitive line that lets them know when they've gone too far. That line is drawn by the parent. Each time the line is crossed discipline must follow. It needs to be quick and consistent. Counting to three over and over or yelling sends the message to the child that it's okay to push the limits. In fact, when discipline is inconsistent, it's no longer discipline; it is abuse. The child doesn't understand why they're being disciplined for an offense when they've gotten away with that same offense on previous occasions. I think the following passage from Ephesians explains it well:

Children, obey your parents in the Lord, for this is right. "Honor your father and mother," which is the first commandment with promise: "that it may be well with you and you may live long on the earth."

And you, fathers, do not provoke your children to wrath, but bring them up in the training and admonition of the Lord. (Ephesians 6:1-4 NKJV)

The last verse governs the first three. Dads, if you do your job with your children they will do what's asked of them in the first three. Train, encourage, admonish, in the Lord. Another way to say this is to say;

"Fathers, prepare you children for adulthood, unprepared children are angry children, but prepared children are a

blessing to their parents and will have a successful life on this earth." (This is my paraphrase)

Our world today is full of angry children, just check the evening news, you hear about them frequently. This stems from a lack of leadership in the home.

Back to the Feeler. The Feeler needs to find balance between their Thinking function and their Feeling function. They must be aware of their tendency to give mercy *carte blanche*.

2. How Thinkers and Feelers prefer to be treated

- ☐ **Thinkers** need to know they're being treated fairly when decisions are made that affect them.

- ☐ **Feelers** need to know that they are appreciated.

Insights on Thinking

What impact does this trait have on relationships?

I have to admit that, as a Thinker, when I feel like I've been treated unfairly, I have a more difficult time forgiving the one who I see as the offender. For example, if I'm up for a promotion and someone else gets it, and I know that I've worked harder than they have, know more than they do, and have been at the company longer, it is difficult for me to accept. This is especially true when the decision to hire someone else seems to have been influenced by some sort of prejudice against me in the mind of the decision maker.

What can Thinkers do to improve their relationships?

We Thinkers must practice what we preach. The acrostic R.E.L.A.T.E comes into play here. People do things for different reasons, and we won't always be treated fairly in life. Having the false expectation that we will always be treated fairly is setting ourselves up for disappointment. We can allow ourselves to go down the path of anger and depression if we choose to, but things will go better for us if we choose not to do that.

If you're a Thinker, learn to relieve your stress level by releasing any expectations you might have in a particular situation, because you can never know how someone else's actions, beliefs, and decision will affect the outcome. Don't allow yourself to expend all of your energy on destructive feelings like anger or depression over someone else's decision. Why should you allow someone else to control the quality of your life? When you first adopt this way of thinking it can be challenging because it involves letting go of a certain measure of control, but it is worth it for the inner peace and resiliency you'll gain as a result.

Life application verse:

> *Do not judge, so that you won't be judged. For with the judgment you use, you will be judged, and with the measure you use, it will be measured to you. Why do you look at the speck in your brother's eye but don't notice the log in your own eye? (Matthew 7:1-3 HCSB)*

Insights on Feeling

What impact does this trait have on relationships?

Linda is very much a Feeler, and as such, she struggles when her dedication and hard work go unnoticed for an extended period. She is very resilient, but I've realized how important it is for her to feel like her efforts are appreciated. When I express words of appreciation, I can see her countenance change, and soon thereafter, her upbeat personality comes to the surface. When a Feeler does something notable, such as spearheads a project or provides a service of some sort, they do it as much for someone else as they do for themselves. A Feeler is rewarded just by knowing that someone appreciates what they have done, especially when that person verbalizes their appreciation.

What can Feelers do to improve their relationships?

Feelers must strive to maintain a healthy perspective on things. If you're a Feeler, this means keeping in mind that people usually don't offer words of appreciation for most things you do in life, and in some situations, there may never be any praise for your efforts. The key to finding happiness and fulfillment lies in doing things for the right reasons. This is why Linda's life verse is so important, especially in this scenario. Let me share that verse with you as well:

Life application verse:

> *Whatever you do, work heartily, as for the Lord and not for men, knowing that from the Lord you will receive the inheritance as your reward. You are serving the Lord Christ (Colossians 3:23 HCSB).*

3. What Happens when Thinkers and Feelers Use the Opposite Function?

- ☐ When **Thinkers** make a decision based on their personal values, they feel as though they're making a biased decision.

- ☐ When **Feelers** make a decision based on logic alone, it feels as though they're leaving out what really matters – the human element.

Insights on Thinking

What impact does this trait have on relationships?

It is impossible for a Thinker to use the *Feeling function* alone when making a decision. A Thinker's mind goes immediately to evaluating the facts, truths, principles, causes and effects of that decision, and so on. When a Thinker goes against their preferred evaluation process and the conclusions they've drawn, it makes them feel as though they've lost their personal integrity. On the other hand, if someone violates their personal values, they tend to justify retaliation unless they have a greater principle to fall back on. (See the life application verse for Thinkers in the previous section, which teaches us how to overcome this tendency toward retaliation.)

What can Thinkers do to improve their relationships?

Thinkers have to make a deliberate choice to use their less dominant Feeling function when faced with a decision. This is something I've learned to do as a Thinker. I have also learned to place a very high value on relationships over the years, and I've gained a deeper understanding of the predicaments people find themselves in, and I have abandoned the phrase, "They made their bed ... now let them sleep in it," something I used to say readily. I have learned to show grace and mercy in order to help a person through a difficult time in their life. Depending on the situation, I am no longer quick to insist on a Thinking evaluation of a situation. I take in a lot more information than I used to, and one of the things I now consider factual is someone else's value system. Their value system is a fact that cannot be denied.

Life application verse:

> *Repay no one evil for evil, but give thought to do what is honorable in the sight of all.* [18] *If possible, so far as it depends on you, live peaceably with all (Romans 12:17 HCSB).*

Insights on Feeling

What impact does this trait have on relationships?

Just as it's impossible for the Thinker to make decisions based on the Thinking function alone, likewise, the Feeler must learn to make decisions using the Thinking function as well as the natural tendency toward Feeling. Their values will enter into their conclusions. For example, if Linda is introduced to someone and all she hears about are the person's achievements in life, she will still ask, "But *who* are you?" She wants to know about that person's family, his or her spouse, kids, what is important to them, and anything that reveals what really makes that person tick. In her estimation, there is plenty of time to learn about their accomplishments. The person matters to her more than whatever it is he or she has accomplished.

Linda and I planted a church in Riverside County and served there for eight years. During our ministry there, we were approached by a young lady who was the founder and director of a small Christian school. She had lost the lease on the building and was scrambling to find a temporary solution for the school. We really didn't have adequate space in our small building to make classrooms for the students, but since she faced having to close the school and we place a high value on Christian education, we told her she could have classes at our church until she found a more suitable building. After spending one year using our church and then planning on using it for the next year, I knew we were about to have a major conflict. During that year, our building began to show the wear and tear of having so many schoolchildren in it on a daily basis. The workers in the church who had to set up for Sunday morning and Wednesday evening services were also feeling this added burden as well. Too often, the school didn't change the classrooms back to service the needs of the church as they had agreed to do. When I contacted the director about terminating the school's use of the building for the next school year, she was infuriated with me. She accused me of being evil and said that maybe I was not even a Christian. She offered no thanks or appreciation for helping her out of her bind in the first place.

The values involved here related to both of us. We were helping children get a Christian education. The facts were that the church was a temporary fix for her situation. She was going to find a more suitable building because the church building was not suitable. She had a lot of time to find another building but didn't bother to look. She placed her values above everything else, including doing her due diligence in finding a home for the school and our values of providing a church for our community.

Did this young woman have good values? Absolutely; no question about it. Did she have the right to override the values of the church with her own values? Absolutely not! She didn't take a single step beyond her Feeling function to make the necessary decisions required with her Thinking Function. She did not look at the facts of the situation, and did not face certain realities that wouldn't go away no matter how much she ignored them.

What can Feelers do to improve their relationships?

It's important for Feelers to learn the value of including the facts, principles, truths, causes, and effects in the evaluation process of decision making. Facts don't have to be cold and heartless. They can provide for you the kind of information that helps you make the most balanced decision. This is especially true when you're involved in a conversation or agreement with a Thinker. It is also important to be careful not to place your values above someone else's.

The life application verse for this issue is actually several verses in **1 Samuel 13:8-15, which** that describe the story of Samuel and Saul.

Life application verses:

> He waited seven days for the appointed time that Samuel had set, but Samuel didn't come to Gilgal, and the troops were deserting him. So Saul said, "Bring me the burnt offering and the fellowship offerings." Then he offered the burnt offering.
>
> Just as he finished offering the burnt offering, Samuel arrived. So Saul went out to greet him, and Samuel asked, "What have you done?"
>
> Saul answered, "When I saw that the troops were deserting me and you didn't come within the appointed days and the Philistines were gathering at Michmash, I thought: The Philistines will now descend on me at Gilgal, and I haven't sought the LORD's favor. So I forced myself to offer the burnt offering."

> Samuel said to Saul, "You have been foolish. You have not kept the command which the LORD your God gave you. It was at this time that the LORD would have permanently established your reign over Israel, but now your reign will not endure. The LORD has found a man loyal to Him, and the LORD has appointed him as ruler over His people, because you have not done what the LORD commanded." Then Samuel went from Gilgal to Gibeah in Benjamin. Saul registered the troops who were with him, about 600 men (1 Samuel 13:8-15).

4. The Different Communication Styles of Thinkers and Feelers

- ☐ **Thinkers** are sometimes told their decisions and the way they express them hurt people, but when the situation calls for it, they can confront difficult matters or people strongly.

- ☐ Sometimes **Feelers** are accused of being too soft in their decision-making, and in their tendency to resist confrontation, but they are good at showing empathy when someone is hurting.

Insights on Thinking

What impact does this trait have on relationships?

Once Thinkers have gathered what they believe to be all the facts and conclude they have the truth generally they will fire the cannon. I know that sounds extreme and sometimes it is. The Thinker can blow away a Feeler in a confrontation and do irreparable damage. I speak from experience. I can recall too many situations from the past that verify an insensitive approach to conflict resolution. I have learned to tone down my approach to proving I've got the facts to make my point. When Thinkers experience conflict with other Thinkers it may sound like a major battle but most of the time things turn out all right for the Thinkers involved in the conflict. Two Thinkers can have pretty heated discussions and still maintain the relationship.

It used to be that I believed Feelers (I didn't know they were Feelers at the time) were very soft and unable to handle the rigors of the competitive business world. Rather than seeing their concern for others as a strength, I thought most of them would cave in under the relational stresses that come with the territory. I had a hard time seeing the importance of compassion and empathy and where it fit into the competitive nature of my world. Obviously, I hadn't tapped into my Feeling function at this point in my life.

What can Thinkers do to improve their relationships?

I give credit to the transforming power of Jesus Christ for the changes that have taken place in my life. I relate to the apostle Paul and his zeal to rid the earth of the followers of Christ when he was still known as Saul, before his conversion. Paul was a Thinker. He would chase them down from city to city. His head was full of facts and justifications for his actions, or so he thought. When he met Christ, all this changed.

Christ not only gives the power to change; He gives the revelation as to *why* we should change. Sometimes He places us in an uncomfortable position that gives illumination into our own blind spots, and in doing so, He empowers us to make needed changes in our lives. I have included a story from my life at the end of this chapter to illustrate exactly what I'm describing here about walking into a situation that is put in your life by God alone.

Life application verse:

> *But speaking the truth in love, let us grow in every way into Him who is the head – Christ (Ephesians 4:15 HCSB).*

Insights on Feeling

What impact does this trait have on relationships?

Confrontation is one of the toughest areas for a Feeler to handle. Feelers are motivated by relationships, especially harmonious relationships, so when they run across someone who is a diehard Thinker, they are baffled as to why they tend to get down to the bottom line of an issue without paying attention to relationship needs first.

A Feeler's tendency is to pull back and avoid being around a person who exercises only the Thinking function. In a work environment, however, a Feeler will find him or herself surrounded by Thinkers and thus will have to deal with them whether they like it or not. Avoiding those who are Thinkers will only perpetuate the discomfort a Feeler has when they're around them.

What can Feelers do to improve their relationships?

Feelers must work on their conflict resolution skills. If a person has a nasty disposition, it's a character development issue, not a personality trait. We never know what someone has experienced in life to make them become the person they are currently. One approach is to make someone like this a personal project, and be as strong, or stronger, than they are in your interaction with them, trying to keep it as lighthearted as possible. I call it mirroring their behavior. My wife Linda who is a Feeler is an expert at this kind of interaction. The tougher the better for her. She will ultimately win their respect and bring about a change in the way they approach her.

It may take a while to perfect this skill, but you can become quite proficient at showing a person (with a nasty disposition) what they look like by mirroring them. If that doesn't work, make it a point to let them know that their behavior is unacceptable to you. Refuse to allow someone to abuse you verbally.

If you have to take a stand against your boss who is mistreating you in this manner, it might cost you your job, which more than likely will benefit you in the long run if he or she refuses to change their approach. I don't think any of us wants to get up every morning feeling as though we're off to the sweatshop to try to earn a living, just to take some more abuse in the process. Life is too short. If you're in this situation, start putting your resume together. Remember, when someone is controlling your emotional life, they're controlling your quality of life as well.

Life application verses:

> *Rejoice in the Lord always. I will say it again: Rejoice! Let your graciousness be known to everyone. The Lord is near. Don't worry about anything, but in everything, through prayer and petition with thanksgiving, let your requests be made known to God. And the peace of God, which surpasses every thought, will guard your hearts and your minds in Christ Jesus.*
>
> *Finally brothers, whatever is true, whatever is honorable, whatever is just, whatever is pure, whatever is lovely, whatever is commendable – if there is any moral excellence and if there is any praise – dwell on these things (Philippians 4:4-8).*

5. How Unresolved Conflicts Impact Thinkers and Feelers

- ☐ **Thinkers** don't like unresolved conflict, but they can survive without harmony.

- ☐ **Feelers** have a tough time with unresolved conflict. Harmony is very important to them.

Insights on Thinking

What impact does this trait have on relationships?

Some people actually enjoy conflict. I'm not one of them. I prefer a harmonious environment, but I have no problem confronting someone when necessary. If I'm in a situation with someone who refuses to deal with an unresolved conflict, I will exercise assertiveness . If the conflict seems un-resolvable however, I do make sure I've worked things out with God. I ask for forgiveness for any wrong that I have done, and I forgive the other person involved in the conflict if forgiveness is necessary. I want to maintain a clean conscience and not carry the weight of unresolved conflict within me.

What can Thinkers do to improve their relationships?

Thinkers need to put focused effort into improving their communication skills. They also need to approach disagreements with an attitude of sensitivity toward the person who has more than zealous concern over the issue; this is especially true when settling disagreements with *Feelers*. If you're a Thinker having a disagreement with a Feeler, try to make them more comfortable in discussing the conflict. Preface what you're about to say with bridging statements such as, "I may have misunderstood what you said (or did); can you help me get some clarification?" Take responsibility for your interpretation of the situation and don't start out by pointing fingers or asking 'why' questions, which sound accusatory and put the other person on the defensive.

Life application verse:

> When a man's ways please the Lord, he makes even his enemies to be at peace with him. (Proverbs 16:7 ESV)

Insights on *Feeling*

What impact does this trait have on relationships?

In my experience, Feelers have difficulty with conflict. Harmony is the desired element in all of their relationships. They will avoid confrontation as long as possible. Sometimes they will even act as though everything is okay while they struggle with the pain of an unresolved conflict. When talking with a Feeler about conflict, I remind them that conflict is not bad; in fact, it is inevitable. Any real relationship that is more than a dime deep is going to have conflicts from time to time. The key is to develop good conflict resolution skills. Confrontation does not have to be painful and uncomfortable if you know how to approach a person with a sincere desire to understand them and make peace with them.

What can Feelers do to improve their relationships?

if you're a Feeler, and oftentimes you seem to be the only one who's feeling conflicted in a disagreement between you and someone else (especially a Thinker), you must work on how to confront them in such a way that builds a bridge between the two of you. Too often Feelers back away from relationships rather than working through the conflicts they have with others. Like the person who prefers the Thinking function, you too must learn to preface the confrontation in any way that will defuse the emotional aspects of the conflict. A good practice is to start the process with prayer before you approach the other person to sort out an issue between the two of you.

Life application verse:

> *Turn away from evil and do what is good; seek peace and pursue it (Psalm 34:14).*

6. The Emotional Characteristics of Thinkers and Feelers

- ☐ **Thinkers** try to screen out any source of emotional pull from their decisions. They focus on the content, the "what" that is involved.

- ☐ **Feelers** focus on personal considerations. Their emotions are a comfortable part of the process. It's difficult for Feelers to focus on the content alone.

Insights on Thinking

What impact does this trait have on relationships?

For most Thinkers, emotions are not a comfortable part of the information they want to evaluate. In fact, many Thinkers would say, *let's not go there at all* when it comes to dealing with others' emotions. That was my way of operating for years. Consequently, I was insensitive to the values and emotional responses of others. I know this sounds arrogant and it probably was, but my typical reaction to emotional responses was to think, *Get over it!* I eventually realized my emotions were an important part of my life too, and that I had been suppressing them for years. In a way, our emotions are the dimension that gives us input concerning likes and dislikes, fear and anger, joy and sadness, and so on. If we take the time to look at the reasons for our emotional reactions, we can make some great discoveries about what we really value.

What can Thinkers do to improve their relationships?

A Thinker needs to be more attentive to his or her own emotional reactions as well as to those of others. Such awareness gives us the ability to connect at a deeper level. I can't stress the importance of this point enough. Everyone has personal values. If I disregard that fact, I'm in effect saying I do not care about what you believe to be true. This attitude will produce many future periods of loneliness for the Thinker and they will do nothing related to advancing the Kingdom of God as they live out their lives in solitude.

Life application verse:

I will meditate on Your precepts and think about Your ways (Psalm 119:15 HCSB).

Insights on Feeling

What impact does this trait have on relationships?

Emotions give insight into the things we value, so Feelers are interacting with their emotions on a regular basis. However, that's not necessarily true for Feelers who have lived in abusive situations for a good part of their lives. Emotions have no chronology. If we give thought to a hurtful memory and dwell on that thought, we will experience the fullness of the emotion all over again. That's one of the reasons people who are locked up in their past tend to experience hopelessness and depression. If you're counseling someone who is a Feeler and who has experienced an abusive past, sometimes they will have a hard time distinguishing the past from the present.

What can Feelers do to improve their relationships?

Feelers sometimes need to take a step back to see if their emotions are having too much of an impact on their decision making process, to the point of overriding rational thought. Otherwise, they'll probably make a decision or respond in a way that they'll regret later. Feelers like to have emotional input, but at some point, they must move closer to the Thinking function to keep from making decisions based on emotions.

Life application verse:

> *May the God of hope fill you with all joy and peace in believing, so that by the power of the Holy Spirit you may abound in hope (Romans 15:13).*

A Short Testimony Related to this Topic

This testimony serves as a good example of how I use my Thinking and Feeling functions. In 1979, I was hired to oversee the Care Ministries of the church I attended. I had a deep desire to help people, and my pastor recognized that about me. He also recognized my administrative skills and thought I could bring some organization and structure to the ministry. He was right about the organization and structure, but I was like a bull in a china shop when it came to counseling, home groups, and relational issues that inevitably cropped up in the care ministries.

Unaware of personality types or temperament issues at that time, I moved forward with my ministry work as best I could. If anyone came to my wife and me for counseling during that time, he or she ended up with an instant seminar on how to change their life for the better. I rarely listened to someone's issue for more than ten minutes before I started teaching them and telling them how to solve their problems. Thank God for my wife, who would graciously interrupt me and nudge me to listen to our counselees. She was listening with an empathetic ear so she could provide some comfort, and I was listening with an ear to figure out how to fix the situation. And so it went, until I received a brochure on a Christian retreat being held at a Christian college, on the topic of understanding human relationships. I signed up and packed my suitcase, and then I loaded a notebook with lots of paper for taking notes and off I went to the retreat while Linda stayed with her cousin in Oakland.

When I arrived on Sunday afternoon, I registered and unpacked my belongings in my room. On Monday morning, I went off to class, eager to fill that notebook with lots of good information. Our retreat leader was a Christian woman close to my age who had two PhDs in Christian counseling and was on the staff at a very well known church in Southern California. I was duly impressed and couldn't wait until she started her lectures. To my surprise there were not going to be many lectures. She started out by breaking us up into groups of seven, and then she said our groups would be called "families." I began to get very nervous. The word "family" sent chills down my spine, because family to me meant chaos and pain. Permit me to take a moment to give a brief overview of what it was like growing up in my family.

I grew up in a family of six boys, of which I was the second oldest. My dad was a hard-working man who owned his own business. He was also an alcoholic. My mother was an alcoholic as well.

I won't take the time to describe the chaotic situations my brothers and I faced over the first fourteen years of my life, but let's just say that all culminated in a very traumatic thing that happened when I was fourteen. My father had been diagnosed with sclerosis of the liver, and the doctor had told him that if he had another drink, it would be over for him. When my parents broke the news to us, it was devastating. Up until this time, I had lived to please my father. He loved sports, so I had worked extra hard at sports in an effort to win his approval.

One day after my father had quit drinking and been sober for six months, and things had begun to stabilize a little bit in our family, I walked into the kitchen to see my father and mother having a drink. I was furious and said to my dad, "If you don't pour out that drink right now, I am going to start drinking." I was trying to shock him into quitting drinking again; I didn't know what else to do at that point. My brothers and I had scolded both of them after we had found their hiding places for their whisky and had poured it out, and we did whatever else we thought would stop them from drinking. I thought maybe if I threatened them with me drinking that would do it.

They both just laughed at me, so I walked over to the refrigerator, took out a can of beer, sat down at the table with them, and drank it. They seemed to think it was cute or something. Meanwhile, I choked it down, becoming angrier with every gulp I took. Two weeks later, I found myself standing next to my thirty-nine-year-old father's casket, staring at him but not shedding a tear. I was angry at him, at my mother, and at God for letting it happen. The uncanny thing is that I started drinking every chance I got, and I didn't stop for sixteen years. I was on the same path he'd been on, and without Christ intervening in my life when I was thirty years old, I probably wouldn't have lasted as long as my dad did.

Before too long my mother's alcoholism brought her to the point of being completely irresponsible as a parent, and all of us boys except for my older brother, who was now eighteen and legally on his own, were sent to Father Flanagan's Boys Town, an orphanage, where we would live out the rest of our childhood.

In my "family group" at the retreat, there were five women, most of who were close to my age; one was a little older and there was a young man who was a youth pastor. When introducing ourselves to the other group members, one of the women said to me, "I'm glad you're in the group because I consider you the enemy." I was taken aback by that statement, but I didn't ask for an explanation. We were given assignments by the seminar leader, and from the very first one I began to consider leaving the retreat. We were asked to draw the dinner table we sat at as a child, and draw in every member of our family, coloring them a different color that would represent something unique about them. I colored one brother yellow because he was happy-go-lucky and nothing seemed to bother him; I colored another one blue because he seemed to struggle with depression; another one I colored red because he was angry most of the time, and so on. It was like taking the lid off the long-buried, painful memories of my childhood, and frankly, I didn't like doing those exercises. Of course, everyone in the group had to do the same exercise, but they seemed to enjoy discussing the painful points in their lives.

In our group discussions, I went into "pastor/counselor" mode and suggested Scripture verses that might help others with their painful memories – all of which were quickly rejected. I began to wonder if I was really at a Christian retreat.

The next day after we did another memory jogger exercise, we went outside onto the campus grounds, sat on the grass under a tree, and began to interact. The woman who had called me "the enemy" had a meltdown based on the way her abusive alcoholic husband, who she was now divorcing after twenty years, had treated her. The air was blue with the descriptive adjectives she was using. I hadn't heard language like that since I was in the business world dealing with angry customers. I decided I would help. I asked Janice (I'm using fictitious names), "Do you realize that your anger is doing more damage to you than it is to him?"

Wow, that did it! She stood up, came over, and got into my face and began to cuss me out, saying, "All you've done since you've been here is give advice! Has it occurred to you that I don't need your advice, but a hug would be very helpful at the moment."

That had never occurred to me. I was stunned. I had honestly thought I was being helpful. Obviously, I had failed miserably. That evening I called my wife who was across the bay and I said, "I'm packing up and leaving the seminar, and not only that, I'm leaving the ministry. I'm obviously incapable of helping people."

Linda in her sensitive way asked me to come and have dinner with her so we could talk face to face. At dinner Linda pleaded with me to see it through because she believed by the end of the week God would make it clear to me why I was there. I agreed to tough it out so I went back.

After our activity on Wednesday, the older, wiser lady in the group, Louise, asked me to go for a walk before lunch. I reluctantly agreed. She gave me some background on the other ladies in the group. All of them had experienced abusive relationships with men, and they saw me as a typical minister who had grown up in a Christian home and attended Bible School and Seminary. In their minds, I didn't have a clue about how difficult life was for everyone else.

I listened in silence. At first, I was surprised they saw me as she described. I sure didn't relate to what she said. Then she asked me if that perception was accurate. Fueled with a little anger of my own, I began to give her some details of my background. I guess we walked and talked for about an hour. When I got to the part about my father's death, for a moment Louise stood there with her mouth open, and then she finally said, "No wonder you hang on to the scriptures like it's a matter of life and death."

To this day, that statement has never quit ringing in my ears. I did cling to the Bible (and still do) for its truth and stability, two things that had been missing in my life for years.

Louise said, "We've got to tell the others about your background." And with my anger still palpable for the abuse those women had leveled on me, I said, "I'm not telling them anything." I figured it was my turn to punish them with my rejection of them.

Louise did go back to the group of women and fill them in, because from that point on they were interested in finding out how I overcame some of my experiences. I was still a little reluctant to share much with them. I approached our interaction very carefully. I must say that by the end of the week, however, we were a bunch of happy campers who had worked through a lot of painful emotional issues together. I had begun to allow myself to process through my Feeling function, which in turn gave me the ability to empathize with the painful life experiences of others.

One other very significant life-changing thing happened on Thursday. After our morning group activity and discussion, I went for a walk with the leader of the seminar. I had arranged for the walk the first day of the retreat, hoping to pick her brain and get a lot of information to take back with me. We had gotten about twenty feet into the walk when Mary said, "I've been watching you this week, and I believe there's a little boy locked up in you that wants out." With that statement, I began to weep like a brokenhearted child. There I was a thirty-five-year-old man in the middle of a Christian College campus with people all around, crying like a baby. Looking back on this later, I realized I had not shed a tear since before my dad had died. The week of digging into my experiences as a child had pulled me through a knothole emotionally, and Mary had hit the nail on the head. This was the grand finale of the week.

We walked to a more private spot on the campus and sat down on the grass. She first prayed with me and asked the Holy Spirit to bring to my remembrance those painful places in my life that needed to be healed, and then to heal me. She asked me to allow the Holy Spirit to take me back to events that actually took place in order for healing and understanding to take place in my life. I had my eyes closed, and I began to see life events pass through my memory like a fast moving slide show until they stopped on one slide. It was me as a four-year-old standing in the doorway of my bedroom. It was about midnight, and I had been awakened by my parents screaming at each other. They were drunk. I saw my mother with a butcher knife standing in front of my dad. I immediately ran to the kitchen where they were and grabbed my mother by the leg, thinking I could forcibly stop her from stabbing my father. She did stop, not because of my strength, but because of my presence. The Holy Spirit revealed that was my last day as a carefree child. I instinctively realized that because my parents were irresponsible, I must become responsible. I have since found out that is part of my inborn temperament. David

Keirsey calls my temperament type the Guardian. Four is a bit young to take on adult responsibilities.

Beyond that event, we went through several other events until we concluded with me standing over my father's casket. Mary asked me what I would like to say to him. I blurted out, "Dad, you hung me out to dry," and with that I began to weep from what seemed like the deepest part of my heart. The Holy Spirit revealed to me that yes, my father had chosen to abandon my brothers and me through the slow process of suicide, using alcohol as the device to do so. But He also showed me the extreme pain and brokenness in my dad and his inability to deal with it on his own, something that is true for all of us – thus our need for a Savior. People who never experience the power of Christ working in their life use some sort of external substance to deal with their pain. I had empathy for my dad like never before. I was able to forgive him for abandoning us.

There were many discoveries for me that day, and one of the biggest was that I had a tool within me that had lain dormant for years, called my Feeling function. From that day forward, the ability to interact with and gain insight from my emotions would change the way I evaluate and set priorities in life.

I also learned to have empathy for others and minister in ways that go far beyond the facts I had learned in a classroom about healing broken relationships. Despite all of the confusion I experienced in the first part of the week, this retreat stands as one of the highlights of my life. It really opened my eyes to a major blind spot in me. I would encourage all Thinkers to work on developing their Feeling function. It will change the way you relate to others in a very positive way. I'm not asking you to throw out the Thinking function and its way of evaluating, but I am saying to bring more balance into your decision making by using both functions of Thinking and Feeling to evaluate.

CHAPTER 8

COMPARING THE TWO ATTITUDES OF JUDGING AND PERCEIVING

Remember, there are two sets of functions used for gathering data: Perceiving (which gathers data using Sensing and Intuition) and Judging (which evaluates data using Thinking and Feeling). These describe how we prefer to perceive, that is, how we gather information, and how we evaluate or make judgments on the information we've gathered.

There are also two sets of attitudes, Extraversion and Introversion and Judging and Perceiving. Both sets of attitudes point to and give us information about which of the functions we prefer to use and how that choice impacts our outward behavior.

The attitudes of Extraversion and Introversion determine whether we process the functions externally or internally. The Judging and Perceiving attitudes tell us which function we use to Extravert, meaning to interact with our outer world, and which function we use to Introvert, meaning to process information internally.

In this chapter we will focus on the Judging and Perceiving functions, which are the functions we Extravert, meaning, how we interact with the world around us. These would be the obvious outward behaviors that are easily recognized by everyone in our lives.

1. The Preferred Living Environments of Judgers and Perceivers

- **Judgers** desire to have the external world organized and orderly. If Thinking is the Judger's preference, they tend to organize processes and structures. If Feeling is their preference, they prefer to organize people.

- **Perceivers** want to experience and understand the world they live in, not organize it. If the person's preference is Sensing, their tendency will be to gather data that can be perceived with their five senses. If the person prefers Intuition, their data will be more abstract and theoretical.

Insights on Judging

What impact does this trait have on relationships?

Like most of the characteristics, Judging can be a double-edged sword. If your friends or co-workers need to have something highly organized they will benefit by getting you involved. Most Judgers will organize things blindfolded while standing on there head. A bit of an exaggeration but organizing and stabilizing is a natural skill for Judgers. On the other hand, Judgers have to be careful that they don't organize all of the fun out of life. My wife, who possesses a Perceiving attitude, has experienced the stifling impact of being so organized by me that there is no room for anything new or unplanned in our lives, and that is what she loves the most: spontaneity.

What can Judgers do to improve their relationships?

As a Judger, I have learned how to plan spontaneity for the sake of my wife's sanity. I organize it by putting it on the calendar, but I don't tell her about it. In the process, I've also learned how to quit taking life so seriously and to lighten up instead, and sometimes the spontaneity just happens. If everything doesn't have a place or isn't in its place, the world is not going to end. So the phrase "lighten up" comes to mind very often.

Life application verses:

> Noah did this; he did all that God commanded him. *(Genesis 6:22 NKJV- read vss. 14-22)*

Insights on Perceiving

What impact does this trait have on relationships?

The Perceiver enjoys most all aspects of their lives. Their outlook is generally positive and they see hope for the future. Most Perceivers have a propensity towards curiosity that drives them on to making new discoveries in life. They are open to see what others are doing and how they are doing it. Life is an adventure. The double edged sword for the Perceiver is their tendency to get so engrossed in experiencing life that they often lose track of time. So being on time to events that are scheduled can sometimes be a challenge. The other issue that stands out for the Perceiver is that they start a lot of projects, get distracted, and don't always finish them. This can be a frustration to those who are relying on them to stay on task and get the job done.

What can Perceivers do to improve their relationships?

Linda counteracts her free flowing style by writing notes in a centralized location on a paper pad. She has disciplined herself to write down dates and times of future events and important projects or phone calls that need to be made. If she writes the notes down on a scrap of paper, there is a good chance of her losing it. The bigger issue is for her to look at it when the day starts rather than responding to whatever comes up and then sitting down at a slow moment in the afternoon and realizing that she hasn't looked at her notepad yet, and something important needed to be handled earlier in the day.

Life application verses:

> *Pay careful attention, then, to how you walk – not as unwise people but as wise – making the most of the time, because the days are evil (Ephesians 5:15-16 HCSB).*

2. What Judgers and Perceivers consider to be a good day

- ☐ **Judgers** are good at making lists and outlining plans. A good day for a Judger is when he or she has completed all that they had planned for that day.

- ☐ **Perceivers** like to be flexible. Lists and plans seem too confining. A good day for a Perceiver is when they've been able to stay busy and have reacted effectively to whatever has come up.

Insights on Judging

What impact does this trait have on relationships?

Judgers wake up with a plan for the day. They may or may not make a physical list, but do have a list that they will be working on throughout any given day. They can get frustrated if they run up against obstacles and changes that keep them from accomplishing those things they've planned.

I am amazed at the number of Judgers that use Day Planners, including myself. Perceivers would benefit greatly by religiously using Day Planners. Most Judgers have a built in Day Planner and could get along quite well without a physical Day Planner.

What can Judgers do to improve their relationships?

Patience and flexibility are two virtues that must be developed by a Judger. Plans are rarely carried out without interruptions or the need to do something that is not on the list. Something will hinder plans from being completed every day of your life. I'm sure all Judgers relate. The sooner a Judger understands this unavoidable reality, the better off they will be. Our stress levels will decrease as we learn to be flexible.

Life application verse:

> But in everything and in every way we show that we truly are God's servants. We have always been patient, though we have had a lot of trouble, suffering, and hard times (2 Corinthians 6:4).

Insights on Perceiving

What impact does this trait have on relationships?

When a Perceiver wakes up, it's a new day, and the first thought their mind is *What shall I do today?* Perceivers generally take things as they come while the day progresses. They may have planned something for the day, but it is subject to change if something better or more exciting comes up. They adjust to changing plans very easily. If married to a Judger the Perceiver may have to fit into the Judgers plans for the day. There must be some compromises from both parties to keep things semi comfortable for both.

What can Perceivers do to improve their relationships?

If you're a Perceiver, it is important to get a hold of the concept of self-discipline. It will serve you well. As opposed to the Judger's potential rigidity when it comes to their plans, the Perceiver needs to develop the virtue of self-discipline. These opposing factors have caused more than one major disagreement in our lives. In fact, these two attitudes rise to the surface every day, and Linda and I have to deal with them like two mature adults. Knowing what we know about these attitudes has helped us understand some of the more frustrating areas of our relationship.

Life application verse:

The wisdom of the prudent is to discern his way, but the folly of fools is deceiving. Proverbs (Proverbs 14:8 NKJV)

3. How Judgers and Perceivers Relate to Others

- ☐ **Judgers** believe they know the most expedient way of doing things, and they don't mind telling others. If the Judger is also a Thinker, they believe they have all the facts necessary to establish a conclusion. If the Judger is also a Feeler, they believe they have had all of the relational experiences necessary to establish a conclusion.

- ☐ **Perceivers** like seeing what others do, and how various processes turn out. **Perceivers** enjoy seeing new ways of doing things. What you'll hear from your perceiving friends is not what they've concluded, but what they've discovered. They will also want to know or share in your discoveries.

Insights on Judging

What impact does this trait have on relationships?

People can rely on Judgers for quick and accurate information most of the time. However, Judgers sometimes come across as a stubborn know-it-all because they are so fast to draw conclusions and then give their opinion. It's especially frustrating to people when they tell them, "This is the way you do that," or, "You can't do it that way." People that I'm in relationship with don't appreciate that characteristic in me. This is normally cured by having to humbly backtrack when someone brings more information to the situation than I had collected. Over the years I have often found myself saying, "If only I had known this or that I would have made a different decision," especially when it comes to relationships. Understanding this information about the Judging preference will help you make healthy adjustments in the way you relate to others and show respect for their unique perspective on life and their way of doing things.

What can Judgers do to improve their relationships?

As a Judger, even though you gather data and make decisions quickly, it's helpful to ask friends what they think before you give your two cents' worth. First, get additional information that could change the way you see things. Second, learn that it's an added benefit in developing relationships as well. The other bonuses are that you make better decisions and expand your world by taking in more information from a variety of sources. Understanding this about the Judger has proved to be a great and enjoyable benefit. My friends enjoy giving their input, and when I choose to enjoy receiving it instead of being bothered by it, it makes for some great interaction between us.

Life application verse:

God resists the proud, but gives grace to the humble (James 4:6).

Insights on Perceiving

What impact does this trait have on relationships?

The person with the Perceiving attitude loves to know what you're doing and how you did it. They love the beauty of nature and animal life. They enjoy having a group of diversified friends. All of these traits are the natural aspect of the Perceiving attitude. The more Perceivers experience, the more they enjoy life. They love life, and that draws a variety of people to them. However, don't ask Perceivers where she would they to have dinner; you'll risk starvation before they make a decision, because in their mind, there are just too many choices of good places to eat!

What can Perceivers do to improve their relationships?

Perceivers need to learn that life doesn't end with the next decision they make. There will always be an opportunity to do something different in the future. So, whenever they are conflicted about which way to go, or what decision to make, just make a decision based on your knowledge of the situation at the time. They are usually happy with the results, but when they're not, they consider it a learning experience. The other positive side to this learned skill is that their Judger friends (and husband!) appreciate them coming to a conclusion in a timely manner.

Life application verse:

> *To everything there is a season, and a time for every matter or purpose under heaven (Ecclesiastes 3:1 Amplified Bible).*

4. Judgers and Perceivers' Approach to Time

- ☐ **Judgers** see their management of time as a decision. It's important for them to be in control of time.

- ☐ **Perceivers** see time in terms of opportunity. Time is secondary to spontaneity.

Insights on Judging

What impact does this trait have on relationships?

Because Judgers have this internal clock running inside of them, they find themselves constantly making adjustments to accommodate time. Their internal clock serves them well for the time-oriented world they live in. The norm for the Judger is to be early to everything, which in turn drives Perceiving companions crazy. If Judgers went everywhere based on the Perceiver's schedule, Judgers would be late to most time-oriented events.

One of the major problems with the Judgers time orientation is that they don't set aside time for fun and relaxation, and I also miss out on developing relationships. For me, as a Thinker who is also a Judger, I don't allow enough free time in my life for people. I'm too focused on process and production. As I've gotten older, I've come to see the error of my ways. People are more important than processes and production schedules. If I were a Feeler, my focus would have been on people all these years, but probably to a fault, and this would have negatively impacted what I accomplished outside of my relationships with others. We must always strive for balance, because our tendency is to overuse the functions we're predisposed to use. Herein lies the benefit of understanding and developing all of our functions.

What can Judgers do to improve their relationships?

Judgers need to take control of their internal clock and not let it control them. Judgers also have to remind themselves to focus on the important things in life and make those things (and people) a priority over their "to-do" lists. If you're a Judger, refuse to allow time constraints to dictate what you will or won't do. If something is important to you and needs to be done, you will get it done. Make sure you don't over commit by putting yourself in situations that overwhelm you because of the time requirements involved.

Life application verse:

> *He has made everything beautiful in its time. Also, he has put eternity into man's heart, yet so that he cannot find out what God has done from the beginning to the end. (Ecclesiastes3:11 ESV)*

Insights on Perceiving

What impact does this trait have on relationships?

Time is something Perceivers use for making the most of opportunities that arise as they live life. They do not have an internal clock driving them to accomplish set goals. Therefore, Perceivers tend to procrastinate about getting things done that they've committed to and that have a deadline. Perceivers sort of drift along until they realize the deadline is fast approaching, and then they're faced with a last-minute rush to finish.

As a Perceiver, Linda is usually pretty good at getting things done using this take-it-easy approach, but if she miscalculates what it will take to actually finish a project, she will be up all night working on it, and sometimes even then she'll be late getting it done. The worst part is when a deadline is missed altogether.

If a Perceiver is working on a team that requires everyone's individual project to be done in unison with other team members' projects, this creates a stressful situation for the Perceiver, and causes the Perceiver's teammates to get frustrated with him or her from time to time.

What can Perceivers do to improve their relationships?

For the Perceiver, I suggest using a planner to highlight upcoming important dates and times, and to start each day by reviewing it. Also, if you're a Perceiver, give yourself plenty of extra time to get to a scheduled appointment, meeting, or get-together with others – more time than would normally be needed to get to those places on time. Checklists are helpful if you will use them prior to the event to pace yourself and keep track of time.

For completing a project with a deadline, you might have a checklist that looks something like this:

- ☐ When is the project due?
- ☐ How long will it take me to complete it from start to finish?

- ☐ Do I have all the necessary tools I need?
- ☐ What are the contingencies involved?
- ☐ Do I have to rely on others for some portion of the project?

For an appointment, your checklist might resemble this:

- ☐ What time do I need to be there?
- ☐ How long will it take me to get ready?
- ☐ How long will it take me to get there?
- ☐ Do I need to pump gas in the car?
- ☐ Do I need to look up directions first?
- ☐ Do I need to eat before I leave?
- ☐ Do I need to feed the dog/cat/bird before I leave?

A checklist such as this may seem very intrusive and rigid for a person whose attitude is Perceiving. If you're a Perceiver, and you're already thinking that you'll never be able to follow a system like this, you'll find that if you do this for a while, you automatically begin to run the checklist through your mind as you're beginning a project or getting ready to go somewhere. Developing a checklist doesn't take much time, and once you get in the habit of making one and reviewing it every now and then to gauge your progress, it will keep you on track.

Life application verse:

> [9] *Besides being wise, the Preacher also taught the people knowledge, weighing and studying and arranging many proverbs with great care. (Ecclesiastes 12:9 NKJV).*

5. How Judgers and Perceivers approach Goal setting

- ☐ **Judgers** focus so much on their plans that they don't allow room for considering new information.

☐ **Perceivers** can be so distracted by new information that they don't finish what they start.

Insights on Judging

What impact does this trait have on relationships?

Every Judger can relate to something I experience as a typical Judger: sometimes I feel as though I have tunnel vision. Like a horse wearing blinders, I can maintain a narrow focus in order to finish a task and not get distracted. This ability does speed up the decision making process. However, I've learned over the years that the fastest decision isn't always the best decision. While gathering necessary information, I can see most of the tangible information, but I tend to miss a lot of unseen information that would be available by putting some thought time into the evaluation process. The NFJ or NTJ may be quick to make decisions on their intuitive hunches and miss some important tangible information that is right in front of their nose. In any case, if the fourth letter of your personality type is "J," your tendency is to get the decision made so that you can move on to the next one.

What can Judgers do to improve their relationships?

A Judger has to get in the habit of seeing the big picture of a situation before making a decision. As a Judger, you most likely prefer to gather tangible information when faced with a problem you must solve, both literally and in your relationships. Learn to move beyond this comfort zone by thinking "out of the box" and seeking creative solutions to problems. The following Life Application Verse is the result of one who takes the "safe" route. I suggest reading the whole parable Jesus sets forth in Luke 19:11-27.

Life application verse:

> *Then another came, saying, 'Lord, here is your mina, which I kept laid away in a handkerchief; (Luke 19:20 ESV)*

Insights on Perceiving

What impact does this trait have on relationships?

Quite the opposite of how Judgers think, Perceivers need to narrow their broad-minded thinking in order to keep them focused on the task or decision at hand. What is typical for a Perceiver is to start out gathering needed information to resolve an issue, but as they consider each piece of new information, they are tempted to go off in a different direction and lose track of the original issue. Someone who is a Sensing-Perceiver (SP) will have a tendency to be carried off into other areas by the *tangible* information they're gathering, and the Intuitive-Feeler-Perceiver (NFP) and Intuitive-Thinker-Perceiver (NTP) will be distracted by their *imagination* or *ideals*. Both methods have value, but at some point, they distract from the decision and the Perceiver becomes overwhelmed with too much information, thus hampering them from making a decision at all.

What can Perceivers do to improve their relationships?

If you're an SP, NFP, or NTP, the important thing to do is discipline yourself to come to a decision by staying focused on the issue at hand and not going off on a tangent in your mind. To focus on the goal so single-mindedly will require a certain amount of effort on your part. Write down your goal and keep it in front of you. Ask yourself, *how will this decision add quality to my life?* For instance, if you want to go on a cruise this next summer and you're not wealthy, you know you're going to have to set aside the money to pay for everything. For a nice cruise, you have to come up with several thousand dollars. Most of us don't have large amounts of money lying around to be able to make a spontaneous decision to go on a lavish vacation. We have to make a plan, save the money, and thus actualize our dream. If going on a cruise is your goal, you must discipline yourself to a budget that includes setting aside some money for the cruise on regular basis. To accomplish any goal, you have to narrow your perspective so the steps you take are in the direction of the goal. Learning how to set (and reach) goals is a necessity for the SP, NFP and NTP, especially short-term goals.

Life application verse:

The light of the eyes rejoices the heart, and good news refreshes the bones (Proverbs 15:30).

6. How Judgers and Perceivers Differ in Their Outlook on Life

- ☐ Judgers are wired to experience life in a structured and orderly fashion.

- ☐ **Perceivers** are wired to experience life in a spontaneous, free-flowing motion.

Living successfully with someone who is the opposite of your personality type requires knowledge, understanding, and appreciation of both your strengths and weaknesses.

Insights on both Judging and Perceiving

What impact do these opposite traits have on our relationships?

Your approach to life marks all that you do. Considering that Judgers and Perceivers have almost opposite outlooks in their approach, this is a huge potential problem area when they must work in tandem, especially in a marriage relationship. Whether your preference is toward Judging or Perceiving, if you're in a relationship with or married to someone who is the opposite, this will be the most consistent source of frustration you experience in that relationship.

Linda and I have been married for over forty years, and we are opposites: I'm a Judger and she's a Perceiver. We have learned how to live together harmoniously by considering the perspective of the other; doing this has helped us get this far without killing the marriage or, for that matter, each other! We have a mutual understanding of each other's unique differences because we've put time into learning about personality types and the peculiarities of human behavior as it relates to our opposite personalities.

You'll benefit from what you're learning here only to the degree that you work on putting your new understanding into practice in your relationships. I am only touching the tip of the iceberg with the descriptions given in this book; there is so much more to learn about understanding personality types and how that knowledge can impact your life.

Our personal library contains several thousand books, and we've read most of them, which demonstrates the commitment we have to learning about healthy relationships. Sometimes it's painful and requires time and great effort to become proficient at relating with others, but if you do nothing about gaining this knowledge and understanding, your relationships with others are probably deteriorating, especially your relationship with your spouse if you're married. Even if it is eroding so slowly that you don't notice it, the deterioration is still taking place. Many couples come to a crossroad in their relationship where they ask themselves, "What happened?" The love they once shared is not there anymore, and neither is the simple joy of being in relationship with one another. Marriage doesn't have to be this way, however. Your marriage will mirror the choices you've made and the energy and time you've put into understanding what it takes to make your relationship work.

In the following section, I will list a few of the things that have improved the way Linda and I live and enjoy our married life together.

What can both Judgers and Perceivers do to improve their relationships?

First, each of us has to define and clearly understand our own tendencies. That may sound funny, but the reality is that most of us don't have a clear understanding of our own predisposed preferences for approaching the many aspects of life. Remember, these tendencies are not bad; they're just different.

When your strengths are pushed to an extreme, they become weaknesses. On the contrary, appreciating someone else's strengths, especially those whose strengths are different from yours, is an area of strength in itself. By gaining an understanding of both my own and Linda's strengths, I'm expanding my capabilities of facing various situations that come up in life. In doing so, I have added much more perspective and a more balanced way to judge these situations. The same is true for Linda, who approaches life in a manner that is opposite of my preference for approaching life.

To implement all of the functions and attitudes available to us, Linda and I have had to learn how to compromise. A marriage or for that matter any relationship will not survive without it. Too many people see compromise as giving in to their partner's way of doing or seeing something, and they end up feeling bitter about having to "give in" to someone else's way of doing things. It's important to come together and talk about compromises until you're content with the outcome; this way, neither one of you will end up feeling bitter. As you're defining your differences, you're also moving closer to one another. You'll find that your life is much more colorful and you'll make better decisions when you willingly seek the perspective your spouse and/or your trusted friends rather than taking on the attitude that you have to get their input just to satisfy them. Conversely, the life of your spouse or friend becomes much more colorful when they accept and integrate some of your perspectives.

The following are some of the things Linda and I have learned and regularly apply in our relationship.

I have learned that it is not necessary or important to have my life so tightly ordered and structured that it doesn't leave room for Linda's spontaneity and changes in direction. In acknowledging and learning to appreciate these characteristics in Linda, I have experienced personal growth in character, and I've seen an increase in my ability to be flexible and spontaneous in a variety of situations that previously I would have rejected.

Linda has learned to appreciate my capacity to order and structure things, and taking this a step beyond my abilities, she has learned the importance of order and structure in life in general.

I have learned that my plans for the day are not more important than interruptions Linda may bring to my day. When I listen to her, it soon becomes obvious that some of her interruptions are God sent and add a sense of quality to my life that I never would have experienced while I had my nose to the grindstone.

Linda has learned to create lists and to order her priorities, and as a result, she has reached some specific goals she has wanted to attain in life.

Much to my surprise, I have learned that I don't always know the most expedient way to accomplish things, and therefore I keep my mouth shut when Linda or someone else has an approach that is different from mine. Even if it ends up that my way would have worked out better, I reject the urge to say 'I told you so'. The goal is not to determine who has the best way of doing things; it is to accomplish a task while working toward reaching that goal together in joy and harmony.

Linda now feels free to introduce her opinion without fear of being belittled or made to feel stupid for even bringing up her idea in the first place. This in itself has been worth the effort (for both of us) to learn about our personality differences.

I am learning to consider new opportunities when they arise instead of rejecting them outright because they don't fit into the time calculations of my original plan, and on occasion, I will re-prioritize the events of my life as a result of those new opportunities or obtaining new information. I have become much more open to change and doing something differently than just the old proven way.

Linda is now more aware of time constraints if she wants to accomplish certain things in her life or if there are goals that we are trying to accomplish together as a couple.

As you begin to recognize and appreciate your differing personality preferences, you will clearly see that compromise becomes easier the more you do it. We also realize the value of each other's perspective. We begin to see how the synergistic effect of using the strengths of each individual at the appropriate times benefits our decision-making, and beyond that, the mutual respect that is developed for our spouse or close friend is increased dramatically.

Life application verses:

By wisdom a house is built, and by understanding it is established; by knowledge the rooms are filled with all precious and pleasant riches (Proverbs 24:3-4).

As you've considered the descriptions of the various personality functions and attitudes over the last four chapters, I hope you've gained a clearer understanding of your own type. If you think it would solidify your understanding, please re-read the sections that are not quite clear to you, as sometimes the second time brings clarity.

As we shift from personality types to temperament types in the next chapter, you will continue to gain insight into your God-given abilities.

CHAPTER 9

INTRODUCTION TO TEMPERAMENT

When you examine the four letters of your personality type, you will see two-letter combinations within them, which determine your temperament type. These are SP (Sensing-Perceiving), SJ (Sensing-Judging), NT (Intuiting-Thinker), and NF (Intuiting-Feeler). These four Temperament types were developed by Dr. David Keirsey who, through his study of temperament theory combined with his study of Isabel Myers' work on personality types, marvelously connected the two models of evaluating different predispositions in a person's personality and temperament.

One other thing that Keirsey did was to add descriptive names to the two-letter combinations. He calls the SP the Artisan, the SJ the Guardian, the NF the Idealist, and the NT the Rational. Each of these names is a general descriptor for all those who fall within each particular temperament group.

The model developed by Isabel Myers gives us the ability to look at the individual elements of our personality by defining the attitudes and functions of the 16 Types. This model is limited, however, because in reality, these attitudes and functions interact with one another to produce what is called our *basic temperament*. Nonetheless, it is helpful to recognize the impact of each of the elements of our personality on our behavior. It is also important to recognize the impact these elements have on our behavior when they are working together within the overall system of our temperament. Both models are valuable to understanding human behavior.

Our temperament is a composite of the various aspects of our personality type working together. Understanding our temperament broadens the perspective we have of our behavior by looking at it from a systemic viewpoint. If you want to delve deeper into each of these theories, I would suggest reading two books to begin with. One is *Gifts Differing* by Isabel Briggs Myers, with Peter Myers, published by Consulting Psychologists Press, and the other is *Please Understand Me II* by David Keirsey, published by Prometheus Nemesis Book Company. These are the two foundational books behind the many personality and temperament models. As I stated early on, the goal of this book is not to explain the theory behind these models but to show you how the practical application of them can help you better understand yourself, your vocation, and especially your relationships.

As we begin to discuss temperament, I need to acknowledge Linda Berens and the impact she has had on my wife Linda and me in helping us understand temperament. Our foundational understanding of this topic has come from attending numerous seminars taught by Linda Berens beginning in the early 1980s. Linda is the founder of Interstrength Associates and the developer of the Interstrength Interaction Styles which give you great insight on how you fit in a work environment or team. She has developed many innovative tools that help people understand behavior and how it relates to one's temperament type. I highly recommend her book titled *Understanding Yourself and Others®: An Introduction to the 4 Temperaments – 3.0*. You can order this book on her website www.interstrength.com. Her discussion about "Temperament Targets" is worth the price of the book alone. In the next few chapters we will discuss Temperament Core Needs and Temperament Strengths and Weaknesses.

INTRODUCTION TO CORE TEMPERAMENT NEEDS

We all have core needs. These are the basic needs of life, including the physical core needs of air, water, food, shelter, and so on, and all of us share these needs. Beyond these are the specific needs that are unique to each temperament type. To varying degrees, we can relate to some of the core needs of other temperament types, but not nearly as much as we relate to our own specific temperament type. Once again, we should be aware of our blind spots – that is, those things about us that others see but that we don't. Too often, we make things difficult in our relationships by being unwilling to believe others when they are bold enough to tell us about characteristics we have that for the most part are negative traits.

In these next two sections, we will look at some of our core needs and some of our strengths and weaknesses, and we will examine what typically happens when our core needs are not met. Since we will be looking at areas of our life that remain the same throughout our life, the approach to achieving balance and stability is a little different. This is where a vibrant faith will make all the difference. Rather than trying to discover alternative methods for meeting your core needs, which could end up doing more harm than good (if not to you, then possibly to others), you will have the opportunity to allow biblical principles to become a living part of your life. Your faith in God and your confidence that He is concerned about your every need is the only thing that without fail will provide peace in the midst of the storms of life. Since each of us derives comfort and correction from the Scriptures on a personal basis, you may find that the Scriptures we reference as a means of helping you achieve balance are not always applicable to your core needs. With this in mind, seek out verses that have always brought comfort, strength, and balance to your life. We will share some examples as we go along.

INTRODUCTION TO TEMPERAMENT STRENGTHS AND WEAKNESSES

Having limitations based on the characteristics of our temperament is not a negative thing. We all have certain limitations because we're all different. None of us operates with all of the Temperament strengths working in us. That's what makes life so interesting. Actually, these limitations are part of God's plan; He wants us to need each other. There are no lone rangers in the kingdom of God.

When we read the fourth chapter of Ephesians (especially verse 16) and the twelfth chapter of Romans (especially verse 6), and the twelfth chapter 1 Corinthians (especially vss. 12-31) we can clearly see that God intends for us to work together using our individual strengths to help each other and to make progress in His kingdom.

Weakness of character drives us to push our temperament strengths (propensities toward certain behaviors) to an extreme, thus causing those strengths to become weaknesses, resulting in problems in our relationships. Weakness of character will always have a negative effect in our relationships. We suffer from character weakness primarily because of the mentality or belief system we developed while our inherent sin nature was alive and well in our life (and sometimes still is), and secondly, from negative life experiences that have not been processed in a positive manner. The good news is that God has made provision for eradicating these problem areas. When it comes to the sin nature, the apostle Paul gives an incredible testimony:

> *For when we were controlled by the sinful nature, the sinful passions aroused by the law were at work in our bodies, so that we bore fruit for death. But now, by dying to what once bound us, we have been released from the law so that we serve in the new way of the Spirit, and not in the old way of the written code (Romans 7:5-6).*
>
> *For in my inner being I delight in God's law; but I see another law at work in the members of my body, waging war against the law of my mind and making me a prisoner of the law of sin at work within my members. What a wretched man I am! Who will rescue me from this body of death? Thanks be to God—through Jesus Christ our Lord! So then, I myself in my mind am a slave to God's law, but in the sinful nature a slave to the law of sin (Romans 7:22-25 NIV).*

Then Paul goes on to explain:

> *The mind of sinful man is death, but the mind controlled by the Spirit is life and peace (Romans 8:6 NIV).*

So, just as there is a law of gravity, there are other laws at work that must be instituted in our life. Without implementing these laws, major character changes, especially in our inherent nature, are impossible. In Romans chapter 10, Paul explains how to make this change in nature possible.

But what does it say? "The word is near you; it is in your mouth and in your heart," that is, the word of faith we are proclaiming: That if you confess with your mouth, "Jesus is Lord," and believe in your heart that God raised him from the dead, you will be saved. For it is with your heart that you believe and are justified, and it is with your mouth that you confess and are saved. As the Scripture says, "Anyone who trusts in him will never be put to shame" (Romans 10:8-11 NIV).

This is a great promise to those who put their faith in the accomplished work of Jesus Christ on the cross and through His resurrection. I made that change in my life in 1973, and I am ever so grateful to my wife (and her praying friends) for loving this arrogant alcoholic into the kingdom of God. You can study all of the personality and temperament models and improve your behavior and relationships to some degree, but it will not improve your relationship with God one bit. Jesus said it best Himself:

I am the way, the truth, and the life. No one comes to the Father except through me (John 14:6).

Once the spiritual aspect of our nature is dealt with, the other area that influences our behavior is our life experiences, both positive and negative. The positive experiences are usually helpful in developing our self-image and confidence. This is true as long as it doesn't carry over into pride and arrogance. Proverbs says:

The crucible is for silver and the furnace for gold, and each is tested by the praise accorded him (Proverbs 27:21 NASV).

Our negative experiences can even provide positive experiences when we choose to allow God to bring healing to our hearts and help us grow through the experience. Those who have reached such a level of maturity that they can allow this to happen consistently in their lives are few.

Just like the fruit tree that has taken a beating from the elements, we need to add something positive to our negative experiences to override the detrimental effect such experiences can have. The damaged tree needs nutrients to restore it to health. So it is with us. The nutrients we need to override the brokenness in our life are found in God's Word. It is tailor-made for each one of us individually.

> *This is my comfort in my affliction, for Your word has given me life ... He sent His word and healed them, and delivered them from their destructions (Psalm 119:50 and 107:20 NKJV).*

Negative life experiences are only half the battle. The other issue is dealing with a faulty belief system. When someone comes into a relationship with Christ and is born again, they are a brand new person.

> *Therefore, if anyone is in Christ, he is a new creation. The old has passed away; behold, the new has come (2 Corinthians 5:17).*

Make no mistake about it: as a Christian, you are a new creation in the eyes of God. You are part of the family of God; you experience a personal relationship with God; you have a new spiritual insight into God's Word; you gain a new ability to communicate directly with God. All of these things are new! However, when you're a new Christian especially, you mind is not yet renewed; your belief system needs some work; and your will, or what I call your "decision maker," needs work. This is because all of those things remain the same within you even when you're born again. There is definitely an awareness of wrongdoing that was not there previously, because every born again believer now has input from both their own born again spirit and from the Holy Spirit, which helps them make discoveries and changes in their life that glorify God and bring about spiritual growth. The biggest responsibility we Christians have is to discipline ourselves to renew our minds and our belief systems with the Word of God.

> *I appeal to you therefore, brothers, by the mercies of God, to present your bodies as a living sacrifice, holy and acceptable to God, which is your spiritual worship. Do not be conformed to this world, but be transformed by the renewal of your mind, that by testing you may discern what is the will of God, what is good and acceptable and perfect (Romans 12:1-2).*

As someone who has been in full time ministry for the last thirty-plus years, I am amazed at how few Christians live and make important life decisions based on God's Word as their ultimate authority and guide. I haven't "arrived," but I know immediately when I am doing my own thing. The Holy Spirit uses the Word I've put in me to help me with godly direction. When decisions are made in opposition to God's will, they bring nothing positive to your life. One of the hardest verses for me to deal with is this passage from the book of John, spoken by Jesus:

> *I am the true vine, and My Father is the vinedresser. Every branch in Me that does not bear fruit He takes away; and every branch that bears fruit He prunes, that it may bear more fruit (John 15:1-2 NKJV).*

Pruning doesn't always feel good, but as a committed Christian, I choose to allow God to prune those areas of my life left over from my old belief system in my pre-Christ days. Once pruned, the new branch will produce fruit worthy of God's kingdom.

As we look at the various temperament strengths and weaknesses, keep in mind that we are approaching a systemic model that will include habits we've developed throughout our lives, both good and bad habits, along with the natural predispositions we're born with. Positive change will take place as we work on our natural inborn temperament predispositions as well as character issues that are formed by what we believe and subsequently do.

If indeed you have heard Him and have been taught by Him, as the truth is in Jesus: that you put off, concerning your former conduct, the old man which grows corrupt according to the deceitful lusts, and be renewed in the spirit of your mind, and that you put on the new man which was created according to God, in righteousness and true holiness (Ephesians 4:21-24 NKJV).

CHAPTER 10

THE SP – ARTISAN

Core Needs

For each of the four temperament types we will examine three core needs. That doesn't mean there are only three core needs for each type, nor does it mean that you will relate 100% to your temperament type's core needs. No one is pure in his or her type. The same thing holds true for temperament models as it does for personality models. Each of us has more than just one single temperament type working within us. There will be some overlap with other temperament types. The question to ask yourself as you study the following sections is *Which of the temperament types do I relate to most?*

The first temperament type we will look at is the SP-Artisan. If your personality type combination is **ISTP**, **ISFP**, **ESTP**, or **ESFP**, your temperament type is SP, or the Artisan. The three primary core needs of the SP-Artisan are as follows:

1. Freedom to act on impulses
2. To make an impact
3. Excitement, adventure, and fun

My wife Linda is an SP-Artisan, so many of the examples given here are based on her needs, and many of the Scriptures presented here have given her peace and stability during stressful times.

☐ CORE NEED: Freedom to act on impulses

Someone once said the SP-Artisan is so tuned in to what is going on in their body they can feel the blood flow in their veins. That may be an exaggeration, but the point is they are very tuned in to their strong physical impulses. Those impulses provide a burst of energy that SPs act on very quickly. They enjoy and respond to all of the colors, tastes, and sounds of life. My wife will outwardly respond to that which she is experiencing. For instance, when Linda is eating, especially when the food tastes really good to her, she vocalizes mmm, mmm, mmm, with every bite. She has no problem sharing the pleasure she is experiencing in the tasty morsels she is eating. Most of the time Linda is completely unaware that she is responding externally to the pleasure she is experiencing inwardly. Every one of an SP's five senses are seemingly supercharged when compared to the other temperament types.

Of course, there is a negative aspect to this. If the SP has had a difficult life and has not developed the kind of character that brings a healthy balance to their lives, these same energy-charged impulses can get them in trouble. Acting on impulses alone can be dangerous for both the SP and the people around them, especially when taking into consideration their other core needs, which are to make an impact in the world around them and to experience excitement, adventure, and fun. Remember, core needs are the areas in a person's life that they will find a way to exercise.

Scriptural principle for this core need:

> *For freedom Christ has set us free; stand firm therefore, and do not submit again to a yoke of slavery ... For you were called to freedom, brothers. Only do not use your freedom as an opportunity for the flesh, but through love serve one another (Galatians 5:1, 13 ESV).*

Source of stress in relation to this core need:

➢ Restraint

For a person who enjoys freely expressing their impulses, a job that requires a lot of restraint will begin to wear on their nerves after a while. Any of us can survive for a while not having our core needs met, but there comes a point when we start feeling the stress of the circumstances or the environment we find ourselves trapped in when it pushes against our core needs. For the SP, stress may come in the form of boredom, rigid procedures, or working for someone who does not appreciate their occasional impulsive responses.

My former perception of this particular core need of Linda's almost cost us our marriage early on. Based on my conservative core needs, I believed Linda over-reacted to things. I would let her know that her extreme reactions embarrassed me at times. Over the first ten years of our marriage, I managed to get everything organized nicely in our household, including the behavior of the family members. As a result, Linda began to change radically. That brings me to the discussion of how the SP-Artisan will respond when put in the stressful environment of being overly restrained.

Reaction to being restrained:

➢ Self-constraint or escape

In a very constraining environment, the SP-Artisan will have a tendency to self constrain to an extreme. They are very aware of their need to respond to what their senses are telling them, and in an effort to conform, they actually self constrain beyond what is required. As a result, their personality changes dramatically. Once lively and responsive they can become zombie like and appear depressed, which in fact they are. They will muddle along in life thinking something is wrong with themselves (when there isn't), all while trying to restrain them from acting on their natural responses to life.

When I discovered that Linda's personality changes had everything to do with my tight control over her life, it broke me. I realized the wonderful expressive woman I loved in our dating relationship had been required by me to change into a woman who withheld her natural, spontaneous responses to life. And in doing so, she lost her joy for life. Once I was aware of what was happening, I repented and asked for forgiveness, and I began to see Linda return to who God had created her to be. It took time – it always does. Trust is earned, and I needed to earn her trust again. Linda had to learn to trust that I would allow her to be who she is, and she had to learn to appreciate her way of reacting to life. When I conquered my urge to constantly be directing and correcting her (which is one of my blind spots), Linda blossomed. Sometimes people never look at their blind spots and continue to hurt the people they love the most.

Scriptural principle for guarding against the urge to escape:

> *But the fruit of the Spirit is love, joy, peace, patience, kindness, goodness, faithfulness, gentleness, and self-control. Against such things there is no law (Galatians 5:22-23).*

☐ CORE NEED: To make an impact

There is something within SPs that drives them to do or say things that leave a lasting impression on others. Most of the time, they don't even know they're doing this. One of the by-products of this tendency is acting, meaning, taking action. SPs, like no other temperament type, will react to life's situations in a way that grabs people's attention. Acting is a natural pathway for the SP. Some have a tendency to be very funny. They see life situations in a funny light and will express them in a way that makes an impact. Many of our stand-up comedians are SPs. I think a good example of an SP is Jerry Seinfeld. He says his shows are about nothing, when in fact they are about situations that would come up in the normal course of a day, albeit with the Seinfeld spin.

Vocabulary is another interesting way for the SP to impact their environment. They are the developers of the languages of the "hood" or the colloquial languages we hear in a lot the song lyrics today. I think the same is true with a lot of country singers and the unique sayings they come up with. One way or another, SPs want to have an effect on others or make an impact, and it's important for them to *know* that they've done so. The best way of explaining the SP's behavior is that they are looking for a response. They want to do and say things in such a way that get a response from family, friends, and all those around them. This is particularly true if the SP also happens to be an Extravert.

Scriptural principle for this core need:

> *He said to them, "Go into all the world and preach the gospel to the whole creation. Whoever believes and is baptized will be saved, but whoever does not believe will be condemned. And these signs will accompany those who believe: In My name they will drive out demons; they will speak in new languages; they will pick up snakes; if they should drink anything deadly, it will never harm them; they will lay hands on the sick, and they will get well (Mark 16:15-18).*

Source of stress in relation to this core need:

- Lack of response from others

The things that cause stress for other temperaments don't have much effect on the SP. The SP's source of stress is unique: SPs get stressed out when they find themselves in a relationship or environment where their antics (or what some would call their craziness) gains no response. I never know what Linda is going to do next to get a response, but I can say one thing: she makes life interesting and fun. When I become so focused on my responsibilities and duties, especially for extended periods of time, to the point of ignoring Linda's efforts to have an impact on me, I see her begin to withdraw. She is stressed due to not getting any attention from me.

When she notices that she isn't having any effect on me, her self-worth begins to deteriorate. I have learned to be more responsive to her efforts if I want to keep our relationship healthy.

Reaction to lack of response from others:

- ➢ The SP simply moves on

SPs need visible evidence that they are making an impact on the relationships in their life, whether those are with people or organizations they're a part of. Otherwise, they will begin to look at other options for getting this core need met.

Scriptural principle for guarding against the tendency to move on:

> *And let the peace of the Messiah, to which you were also called in one body, control your hearts. Be thankful. Let the message about the Messiah dwell richly among you, teaching and admonishing one another in all wisdom, and singing psalms, hymns, and spiritual songs, with gratitude in your hearts to God. And whatever you do, in word or in deed, do everything in the name of the Lord Jesus, giving thanks to God the Father through Him (Colossians 3:15-17 HCSB).*

☐ CORE NEED: Excitement, Adventure, Fun

Linda and I live in Southern California, and her favorite outings are to the Wild Animal Park in Escondido, or the San Diego Zoo. She could go to both several times a year and maybe even more. She loves animals, and her ultimate desire would be to see them in their natural environment. My experience is that most SPs love animals. My own theory on this is that animals, especially wild animals, reflect many of the characteristics of the SP themselves. SPs desire to be able to roam free and independent from rules and regulations. The adventure of being in the wild, the fun that is experienced as they run into the unknown surprises that might occur, and their instinct to respond using their incredible impulses all fit the SP very well.

You'll find SPs working in the kind of vocations that will challenge their core needs: firefighting, law enforcement special forces, military special forces, fighter pilots, forestry service, and they make some of the best sales people you'll find as well. All of these vocations are not exclusive to SPs, but SPs are attracted to them because of their core need package. You'll find all other temperaments in these vocations as well, but they usually move toward jobs within those vocations to which they are more suited. For example, within these careers, you'll typically find SJs in administration, NTs as commanders or CEO's, NFs in the people-helping departments, but the SP wants to be where the excitement is.

Scriptural principle for this core need:

> *But you will receive power when the Holy Spirit has come upon you, and you will be My witnesses in Jerusalem, in all Judea and Samaria, and to the ends of the earth (Acts 1:8).*

Source of stress in relation to this core need:

➤ Idleness

The SP is stressed by idleness. They have to be busy doing the kinds of things that stimulate their core needs. Looking back to my grade school days, I can pick out the SPs in my class. They were the ones who were bored with the redundancy of multiplication tables and the many things we had to memorize. Whenever boredom set in for the SPs in the classroom, things would always get exciting. Many SPs get through the educational system by the narrowest margins if they get through at all. Sometimes I wonder why we don't educate based on learning styles and interests rather than subjects. I think we would see many more students, especially SPs, get through the educational process more successfully if we did.

Reaction to the stress of prolonged idleness:

➢ The SP shuts down

When SPs are stuck in a boring environment for an extended period, they will shut down. SPs live in the moment, and one of the most challenging things for them to learn is that there will be times and seasons in life when their core needs are not being met, and they must "soldier on" during these times if it means fulfilling their responsibilities because others are depending on them.

Scriptural principle for guarding against the tendency to shut down:

When they observed the boldness of Peter and John and realized that they were uneducated and untrained men, they were amazed and knew that they had been with Jesus (Acts 4:13 HCSB).

☐ STRENGTH: SPs are skilled with their hands

Now we will look at some of the SP's strengths. The first strength of most SPs is that they are skilled with their hands. They tend to be excellent craftsmen. They are the master of the tool. This makes them expert chefs with their superior taste buds and their ability to create a beautiful plate; craftsmen with a great eye and knack for using tools with precision; skilled seamstresses who create beautifully detailed quilts and clothing; and interior decorators who have a knack for combining colors to bring out the best features in the room.

This is why Dr. David Keirsey calls SPs the Artisans. SPs make whatever they are doing artistic, even when it comes to sports. The SP temperament type dominates the world of extreme sports and anything that requires rapid-fire impulsive reactions, danger, and fun. When their senses are stimulated, they will react.

In my younger years, I raced motorcycles. I would go as fast as I possibly could across the California desert or the TT track where I was racing, but what I see these young men doing today with their highflying competitions is beyond anything I can comprehend. I believe the vast majority of them are SP Artisans who have made an art of jumping from a ramp. Considering the core needs of the SP-Artisan, which are acting on impulse, making an impact and experiencing excitement, adventure and fun whenever possible, it becomes clear to see that any form of extreme sport is being done by an SP. This kind of activity also satisfies their natural ability to be masters of the tool, which in the case of extreme sports is their motorcycle, snowboard, or skateboard.

When taken to an extreme, a strength becomes a weakness:

➢ SPs can be so involved in the moment that they miss what's coming next.

To be a true Artisan requires focus. Too much of a good thing can be detrimental to anyone. With the SP, if something catches their interest, they can get into it almost to the point of obsession. Of course, if any of us turn our attention to any one thing for an extended period of time, it means we're missing some other things that are going on around us. If you're a friend or the spouse of an SP, you can probably relate to their single-mindedness when they are involved with something that keeps pulling them back to it. You may begin to feel you've lost a friend or loved one at certain times. The other aspect of this is that the SP needs to be careful that they don't hinder themselves from fully developing other character traits and skills that would serve them well in life, such as learning to balance their checkbook, advancing their education in a specific field of interest, or studying the Bible to grow in their Christian faith. These types of endeavors involve long periods of focused study, something SPs usually avoid whenever possible. Being a master of the tool or a craftsman is a good thing, but investing time in relationships to learn what others like or have an interest in is also a good thing.

Life principle for keeping this strength in balance:

> *Be diligent to present thyself approved to God – a workman irreproachable, rightly dividing the word of the truth (2 Timothy 2:15).*

☐ STRENGTH: SPs work best in crisis situations

Do you remember the television show MacGyver? Angus MacGyver was the problem solver for the fictional Phoenix Foundation in Los Angeles. He was unique in that he preferred non-violent solutions to the various situations he faced. He was an easy-going man, but an extremely resourceful secret agent. Every week he found himself in a crisis that required a quick response; otherwise, he was doomed. With his ever-present Swiss Army knife and anything else he could get his hands on, he would find a way to get out of the fix he was in. He usually only had minutes or even seconds to respond to his dangerous circumstances.

MacGyver is the very definition of an SP-Artisan. If I'm in a crisis, especially a physical crisis, I want my SP friends around me. They are quick to respond to a crisis and will use any resources available to them to bring it to a resolution. Most of the time they aren't thinking anything through; they are simply responding impulsively to the situation, but their natural abilities and skilled hands will diffuse the crisis situation in no time at all.

When taken to an extreme, a strength becomes a weakness:

> ➢ SPs may create problems if there are none to solve

If an SP is in the vicinity and no crisis is taking place, just wait a while and soon there will be one. SPs along with NT's love pulling pranks on their friends. In fact, the first time you meet them they may do something to make a lasting impression on you. Sometimes this can be very irritating to those around them. SPs must remember there is a time and a place for practical jokes, and most situations are not the best for pulling a successful prank on a friend, relative, or colleague. A good prank at the right time is fun for all, but being mischievous at the wrong time usually hurts rather than helps a relationship.

Life principle for keeping this strength in balance:

Pay careful attention, then, to how you walk – not as unwise people but as wise (Ephesians 5:15).

☐ STRENGTH: SPs are good at and enjoy adapting

Two of the temperament types are often referred to as chameleons: SP–Artisans and the NF-Idealists. Both blend very well, but for different reasons. (We'll discuss the NF-Idealist when we get to that chapter.) SPs are very flexible and usually go along with change without a lot of resistance. Once again, this is rooted in their core needs. They enjoy things that are new and exciting. They also love to see new ways of doing things. They don't get hung up with the "if it ain't broke, don't fix it" syndrome of the SJ. You will find that SPs make good team members because of their energy and ability to embrace change, as long as you can keep them from getting distracted.

When taken to an extreme, a strength becomes a weakness:

> *SPs are easily sidetracked*

Because the SP enjoys change and likes to see new ways of doing things, they also find themselves getting distracted easily and having a hard time staying on task. It takes a lot for them to maintain focus and see things through to the end. I can be in my office working on something when Linda comes in and asks me if I would like something cold to drink. My response is yes, thank you, I would like something to drink. About 45 minutes later, I'm sitting there thirstier than ever, still anticipating that cold drink when I realize that 45 minutes have passed. Knowing my wife well, I get up and go into the kitchen to get something to drink, and on the way, I pass Linda, who is now working on her scrapbooking. She *had* fully intended to get me a cold drink, but when walking back to the kitchen after asking if I wanted a drink, she was distracted by something she saw on her scrapbooking table. This SP distinction can be a point of frustration in a friendship or marriage because SPs are so easily distracted by something they need to do on the way to doing something somewhere else. What they were distracted by is usually important, but the problem is they said they would accomplish something else first. They are usually very productive, but finishing what they start is a definite challenge for SPs. Frustration sets in when you think the SP is going to accomplish something for you and it doesn't happen.

Scriptural principle for keeping this strength in balance:

> *Let your eyes look forward; fix your gaze straight ahead. Carefully consider the path for your feet, and all your ways will be established. Don't turn to the right or to the left; keep your feet away from evil (Proverbs 4:25-27).*

☐ STRENGTH: SPs are very resilient

I have observed that SP-Artisans are very resilient and can bounce back easily when they suffer losses or defeat of some kind. They seem to be able to grieve and quickly move on. This ties in to their ability to adapt to new situations and environments. Typically, you won't find SPs rehearsing the trauma or negative experience over and over again in their minds.

Living in the moment is another characteristic of the SP, and this too is a help when it comes to recovering quickly from loss or disappointment. A new day has come with all of its challenges and joys, and the SP has moved on. This does not mean that SPs don't have feelings. When Linda experiences a loss, she has a very strong emotional response. But generally, she doesn't stay in that deep emotional place for an extended period.

When taken to an extreme, a strength becomes a weakness:

> ➤ Sometimes SPs do not fully process things emotionally.

My experience with Linda has been that she sometimes moves on too quickly after experiencing a loss. Then, sometime in the future, out of the blue, she will be feel the full effect of that grief. It may be different with other SPs, but I know from much experience in counseling that if we don't give ourselves time and freedom to grieve a loss, it will hinder our ability to interact with our emotions in a healthy manner.

Scriptural principle for keeping this strength in balance:

Answer me when I call, O God of my righteousness! You have given me relief when I was in distress. Be gracious to me and hear my prayer! (Psalm 4:1 HCSB).

☐ STRENGTH: The SP is a super realist

With all of the SP's flexibility and adaptability, they are also the Super realist. If they don't experience something with their five senses they can be cynical about the information. Show me, would be the SP's typical response. When I think of Bible characters the one that comes to mind is Thomas. It was he that had to touch the scars of Jesus before he believed. Peter was also an individual that lived out his impulses, and he swore he would go down fighting with Jesus and probably would have if there was a fight, but because there wasn't and Jesus was apprehended Peter became confused and subsequently denied knowing Jesus three times. Peter had trouble believing the whole idea of the resurrection. It took the empty tomb to bring him around.

When taken to an extreme, a strength becomes a weakness:

> ➢ *SPs may become cynical*

Cynicism doesn't work well for the person of faith. For the SP, "calling those things that are not, as thought they are" – living in faith – can be a challenge. If SPs don't experience something with their senses, they have a hard time believing it could be true.

So we are always of good courage. We know that while we are at home in the body we are away from the Lord, for we walk by faith, not by sight (2 Corinthians 5:6-7).

A few more characteristics of the SP–Artisan:

- Population of the SP-Artisan in the United States: 38%

- Leadership Style: The SP is a tactical leader; they're great at making decisions in the heat of the battle.

- Time Orientation: The present; the here and now.

- Independent: S's value their independence. It ties into their core need of freedom, adventure and fun.

- Population in the organized church: The population of SP's in the church is very low; my guess is in the range of 5% to 10%. This is my own observation after working in the full time ministry for 30-plus years and doing innumerable seminars using the Myers Briggs Type Indicator and other assessments that measure and categorize types. And many SPs are in church only because they're married to someone who is of another type and who desires to be in church. Linda and I can validate that based on our 22 years of teaching at Youth With A Mission bases: in class sizes of about 30 people, we rarely have more than 3 or 4 SPs in the class. And YWAM's way of doing things is much more conducive to drawing SPs than the typical method of doing "church" is. YWAM's way is very action-oriented, something that usually appeals to the SP: Approximately three months of classes are followed by six weeks of outreach in some remote region of the world. This is definitely a hands-on, practical application of the Great Commission and SP's look forward to that new experience.

When the SP looks at the church, the picture they get is a place that's boring and restrictive, full of do's and don'ts. They are not the least bit attracted to the church. Churches that are making headway with SPs are offering unique, new and exciting ways of presenting Christianity. You must also take into consideration that out of the four temperament types, the SPs are the least spiritual. However, along with the SJs, who also make up about 38% of the US population, they are one of the two largest population groups in the United States. Based on these statistics, it seems to me that the church needs to re-evaluate the way it evangelizes unreached people, considering that the current methods being used are missing the mark with a vast number of people. Just by doing church the way it's always been done traditionally, Christian leaders and ministers are turning off a huge part of the population. Churches are traditionally structured by (and for) the SJ temperament type, which we will look at in the next chapter.

Chapter 11

THE SJ – GUARDIAN

CORE NEEDS

The second Temperament Type is the SJ-Guardian. If you scored ISTJ, ISFJ, ESTJ, or ESFJ, your temperament type is SJ-Guardian. The three core needs of this temperament type are as follows:

1. The need to belong or have membership
2. The need for stability
3. The need for responsibility or duty

Out of all the temperament types, the SJ usually relates more quickly to the descriptions of their personality than other types relate to theirs. The scriptures used in this chapter are mostly verses that have helped me bring balance into my life as an SJ-Guardian.

☐ CORE NEED: Belonging and membership

SJs spend their lives serving the organizations and institutions to which they belong. It can be a church, their workplace, social or service clubs, charitable organizations, and any number of other groups. The need to belong, and being a member of an organization is deeply imbedded in the SJ. The catch is that they don't want membership to be given to them *carte blanche*. They feel a strong need to earn their membership. Becoming a part of the group through serving is a must for SJs. You'll find that SJs are the glue that holds most organizations together. They will set up the rules and procedures and fill needed positions to make things work.

The same is true in relationships. The SJ is a great partner because you can count on them to do what they say they're going to do. This is not true, however, when they have gotten so involved in so many things that they find themselves in overload, or if they feel like their efforts are not being appreciated. If this is the case, they will let you know how valuable they've been to you by not doing the thing that they have done without missing a beat for so long.

Scriptural principles for this core need:

But now God has placed the parts, each one of them, in the body just as He wanted (1 Corinthian 12:18).

So then you are no longer foreigners and strangers, but fellow citizens with the saints, and members of God's household (Ephesians 2:19).

Source of stress in relation to this core need:

> When they or their efforts are rejected

When the SJ senses or actually experiences rejection, the wheels come off the otherwise smooth-running relationship or organization. Rejection can come in many forms, and it all has to do with the SJ's perception and how secure the SJ is. If the SJ is the man next to the chief and the chief brings someone else alongside to serve as his right-hand man, the SJ can take that as rejection. If the SJ serves for a long period of time without any recognition for their efforts, they can take that as rejection. In marriage, when a conflict takes place and the SJ's spouse rejects them, the conflict becomes very hard to resolve because of lack of cooperation from the SJ. What they perceive as rejection is a major stressor for the SJ.

Reaction to rejection, perceived or real:

> ➢ To reject others

"I'll show you!" is the cry of the SJ, or, "You're going to miss me when I'm gone!" Even if these words are not spoken, people close to the SJ will feel the full force of their fury at being rejected. The SJ comes across as short, tense, and biting in their communication. They can quickly adopt the mindset of, "If you don't need me, I don't need you," and if it gets to this point, this could be the end of the relationship, whether it is a friendship or a relationship with a club or institution. The SJ's need to belong is a wonderful trait for everyone around the SJ to experience when things are going well. The SJ will be your best resource, especially when you need someone who is adept at handling logistics. This is true of SJs whether in the workplace or in a personal friendship. The SJ will work harder and be more committed than any other temperament type. They can be loyal to a fault. It's important to let the SJ know every once in a while that their efforts are appreciated.

If you're an SJ, it's important for you to recognize that you have this blind spot; that is, how this rejection issue works in you. Too often, you will misread a situation and take it as rejection (even when it isn't), and when you do, the cycle of rejection will begin.

Scriptural principle for guarding against rejecting others when you think they've rejected you:

> *Since you put away lying, speak the truth, each one to his neighbor, because we are members of one another. Be angry and do not sin. Don't let the sun go down on your anger, and don't give the Devil an opportunity (Ephesians 4:25-27).*
>
> *Bless those who persecute you; bless and do not curse (Romans 12:14).*

☐ CORE NEED: Stability

The SJ's core need for stability works to benefit the whole world. Growth and health take place in a stable environment. Doctors won't do surgery if someone's vital signs are not stable. If the weather is not stable, the space shuttle *Discovery* is not launched. If the economy is unstable, investors hold on to their money until things begin to stabilize. SJ-Guardians were born to bring stability into unstable situations where chaos reigns. The SJ will draw on every possible resource to fix what's broken, to replace what's missing, or to correct problems and direct others by using standard operating procedures or systems to bring about positive results and a predictable outcome.

If you are experiencing instability in almost any environment outside of relationship instability, the SJ is the temperament type that can see the details and gather together the needed information and elements to take the chaos out and put stability into the situation.

However, SJs can be a big part of the instability in relationships. I am a classic SJ; remember my need to stabilize my family? People cannot be managed the same way systems can, and STJs in particular need to realize that relationships operate much differently than the processes and production goals of their vocations, and thus they have to put some time and effort into learning what makes relationships stable. SFJs are more naturally relational, but they also have the same narrow viewpoint of what it takes to fix something, even in relationships.

Most SJs, unless they learn otherwise, do what they think is the right way to do things. That's not bad in and of itself, but the danger lies in the tendency to believe that their way of bringing stability to a situation is the only way. It's a narrow approach to problem solving. When it comes to accomplishing a task and keeping things running smoothly, the SJ usually observes one right way to do it. The "J" part of their temperament emphasizes the bottom line – they want to bring the problem to a resolution and move on. Once they do solve the problem efficiently and nearly flawlessly (of course), they have to fight the compulsion to announce, "It's fixed now – please leave it alone!" This is good for level one stabilization of a situation, but it's important for the SJ to remain open to tweaking whatever they have put in place if they want a system that remains progressive and stays up to date with technological advancements. The SJ works in the here and now and does not see future trends very well, so it is a hard pill for them to swallow to admit that their solution may not be *the* perfect solution forever. But once they do accept this, they will begin to see the advantages of staying open to change.

One other important issue for the SJ is to understand that stress is the driving force behind their core needs. That may sound peculiar, but SJs live with stress simmering beneath the surface constantly. For the SJ, everything they are involved in has a deadline, even if it is manufactured by themselves. Without a deadline, tasks are not taken seriously by the SJ.

Scriptural principle for this core need:

> *Therefore, everyone who hears these words of Mine and acts on them will be like a sensible man who built his house on the rock. The rain fell, the rivers rose, and the winds blew and pounded that house. Yet it didn't collapse, because its foundation was on the rock (Matthew 7:24-25).*

Source of stress in relation to this core need:

➤ Instability

Environments that seem chaotic to the SJ will increase the SJ's stress levels enormously. I say *seem* because SJs are production oriented and thus are always looking to get things accomplished. Careers in research and development do not offer the best working environment for the SJ, because the work is ongoing with no deadline in sight. But in my experience, I've found that many work environments need some detailed, focused SJ input to make things operate more efficiently.

The SJ's reaction to the stress of an unstable environment:

➤ Fix it, and if they can't fix it, leave it

If the SJ is not allowed to help stabilize the environment and it remains chaotic for an extended period, the SJ will begin looking for a more stable environment in which to contribute, grow, and flourish.

Scriptural principle for guarding against the tendency to want to leave:

> *So we must not get tired of doing good, for we will reap at the proper time if we don't give up (Galatians 6:9).*

☐ CORE NEED: Responsibilities and duties

Some people like the unencumbered flowing style that allows them to be free of responsibilities so they can do what they enjoy without any repercussions. That does not describe the SJ. They would look at that approach to life as irresponsible. The SJ seeks out responsibility. It is a value that they hold near and dear, and they think everyone else should do so as well. Whatever is assigned to them as their responsibility is guarded at all costs. Thus, Keirsey calls SJs the Guardians. This title includes all aspects of their core needs. They guard the relationships and institutions they belong to; in other words, they guard whatever they stabilize, and whatever is within their area of responsibility. They also look to their authority figure for direction, and once they have it, they go to work diligently carrying out the task they've been given, quickly and efficiently.

Scriptural principle for this core need:

> *Slaves, obey your human masters with fear and trembling, in the sincerity of your heart, as to Christ. Don't work only while being watched, in order to please men, but as slaves of Christ, do God's will from your heart. Render service with a good attitude, as to the Lord and not to men, knowing that whatever good each one does, slave or free, he will receive this back from the Lord (Ephesians 6:5-8).*

Source of stress in relation to this core need:

> Insubordination

When the SJ observes "rule breakers" and those who shirk their responsibilities, they become irritated and their stress levels increase. Even if the behavior doesn't have anything to do with something the SJ is involved in, they still get irritated. Watching the evening news is not the best way for an SJ-Guardian to unwind; it causes them great frustration just hearing about all of the irresponsible people committing crimes and looking for a "free ride," whether it be by beating the system or forcefully taking what doesn't belong to them. My wife has to tell me to chill out on a regular basis while we're watching the evening news.

The SJ's reaction to the stress of insubordination:

> They begin to make judgments about others

The SJ responds to this kind of stress by making judgments on those who don't seem to be fulfilling their responsibilities. It starts in the work place and carries over into every other area of their life, their family, others' families, their neighbors, and so on. They set up court, and then convict and sentence others whom they deem irresponsible in one fell swoop.

It may sound like I'm especially hard on SJs, but keep in mind that I'm an SJ-Guardian. It's because of my frustrations with myself, and my acute awareness of the things I was unwilling to look at in my own life in years past, that cause me to know so well how an SJ's strengths can quickly turn into weaknesses. I've had to come to grips with this imbalance in my life. I got so tired of going to God and asking forgiveness for my judgmental attitude that I finally began to get some breakthrough in this area of my life. I finally got to the place where I ask God to help me see people the way He sees people, and it works. Relationships are more important than processes and production schedules.

Scriptural principle for this reaction:

Do not judge, so that you won't be judged. For with the judgment you use, you will be judged, and with the measure you use, it will be measured to you (Matthew 7:1-2).

☐ **STRENGTH: SJs are skilled at setting and accomplishing goals**

More than any other temperament type, the SJ-Guardian is very good at setting short-term goals. This relates to the list making that SJs do on a daily basis. Everything they do is linked to the infamous TO-DO list whether it's an actual written list or one the SJ carries around in his or her mind. When the SJ rises in the morning, one of the first things on their mind is *what do I have to do today?* From that moment on, the goal setting begins, and heaven help anyone who gets in his or her way. That might be an exaggeration, but SJs take their daily goals very seriously. In a perfect world, they would accomplish their short-term goals every day.

When taken to an extreme, a strength becomes a weakness:

➤ SJs can become so involved in the moment that they miss what's coming next

The SJ Guardian's tendency to focus so intently on immediate needs causes a void in looking down the road to see what may be coming. This tendency hinders them when it comes to setting long-term goals. They're very busy in the here and now. It's important for the SJ-Guardian to put long-term planning on their short-term goal list so they will set aside some time to dream of the future and plan where they want to be five years down the road. Then they need to set some short, intermediate, and long-terms goals that will get them there. The dreaming part is hard for the SJ also. As an SJ, I have learned the value of dreaming, that is, looking off into the future and establishing a vision of something I want to accomplish or experience, complete with long-term goals. If the SJ doesn't dream a little bit, and then use their goal- and list-making skills to formulate a plan to make those dreams become realities, they will be doing the same thing they are doing today five years down the road. And so it goes.

Scriptural principle for keeping this strength in balance:

Where there is no vision, the people perish (Proverbs 29:18 AEV).

☐ STRENGTH: SJs strive to create an orderly, stable environment

With every new position I've held throughout my life, I've started out by determining what I could do to make it more efficient and stable. This was especially true in my years in the business world. To the SJ, efficiency and stability go hand in glove. They will look at the steps involved from start to finish to produce something, to sell a product and move it through the warehouse and get it to the customer, or even to teach and train people to do a job easier and faster or to learn something in a systematic fashion.

For the SJ temperament type, this is a very positive trait. Every organization needs an SJ to help bring efficiency and stability to the way things are done, because efficiency and stability mean increased productivity and those profits, even if it's a charitable organization. Understanding the Myers-Briggs personality types and the temperament traits, and then hiring the right people for the jobs they're suited for, can be invaluable to a manager or CEO in a business or any organization.

When taken to an extreme, a strength becomes a weakness:

> ➢ SJs tend to over-guard the environment they've created

Once the environment is changed (corrected, they would say), and the new procedures are set in motion, the SJ's message to everyone is, "Don't mess with it." The SJ has a strong tendency to over-guard their new stabilizing procedures. People who mess with the SJ's new system of efficiency are liable to catch the wrath of the SJ who created it.

Even before I knew anything about the MBTI or Keirsey's temperament types, I realized that some people would consistently do things differently than I would. Trying to get them to march to my beat was near impossible. Even if I did, I would eventually lose them because they would be so unhappy about being forced into the mold I had created for them. Experience taught me to lighten up on the way people do things and focus more on their results. If the job was finished in a timely manner, it wasn't all that important how they did it.

Scriptural principle for keeping this strength in balance:

Commit your works to the LORD and your plans will be established (Proverbs 16:3).

☐ STRENGTH: SJs are skilled at standardizing policies and procedures

To assure that everyone understands how things should be done and everyone is on the same page, the SJ-Guardian will create the pages. Pages of the Standard Operating Procedure Manual, that is, and this manual will be done in great detail including the sequential steps that should be followed to complete a certain task. In my experience, I'm not sure anyone ever reads these manuals, but if a question ever arises, the manual is there. Sometimes I think the SJ who writes the manual is the one who benefits most because it is a great way to organize and confirm their thoughts. Most of the time when new employees are trained, they are done so verbally and experientially and not by reading a manual.

When taken to an extreme, a strength becomes a weakness:

> ➤ The SJ can be very rigid concerning the "right" way to do things, and often wants to punish the rule breakers

This is an area to which every SJ-Guardian should pay close attention. I can relate to that compulsion to "punish the rule breakers," and early on when I occupied some of my first supervisory positions, I could be pretty harsh with people who didn't comply with the rules. I soon learned that *form* (rules) should never override *function*. Form is created to help with function. When function is required to serve form, you will begin to kill *purpose*. Form and function are there in the first place to accomplish a purpose and hopefully to do so efficiently. But when you begin to serve form, it's like putting yourself under the law.

When the apostle Paul was speaking to the Corinthian Church about how they were to function in their relationship with God, he warned them against doing this very thing. The Corinthian Church was trying to establish their relationship with God by keeping the Law (form). Paul in essence was saying, 'you'll fail because you are not adequate to do that'. The only one who is adequate is Jesus. Trying to function in relationship with God by keeping the Law will eventually kill the relationship.

As stated in Chapter 6, *The letter of the law kills the spirit*. This principle is so true. This is what Paul was speaking about, and it applies to all standards that are imposed on others. The letter can be Standard Operating Procedures or even unmovable expectations – anything that is written on tablets of stone, even if those tablets reside in our minds.

At this point, I need to say that everyone struggles in this area, not just SJs. This is one of the most important principles we can learn regarding all of our relationships. We need *form* to a certain extent, that is, guidelines for healthy relationships, but when we expect others to serve the form (law) we kill the relationship. Before making judgments against others in our hearts and minds, we must infuse all of our thoughts with the Spirit. Notice the word Spirit in the passage is capitalized. It's the Spirit of God that will show us how to handle what we see as insubordination or rebellion in others. Once I learned this truth, it revolutionized the way I related to others.

Scriptural principle for keeping this strength in balance:

> *Not that we are adequate in ourselves to consider anything as coming from ourselves, but our adequacy is from God, who also made us adequate as servants of a new covenant, not of the letter but of the Spirit; for the letter kills, but the Spirit gives life (2 Corinthians 3:5-6).*

☐ **STRENGTH: The SJ is a giver, a server, and a caretaker**

You will find that the highest percentage of workers in most churches are SJ-Guardians. They are ushers, Sunday school teachers, greeters, parking lot attendants, those who set up the chairs and put them away again, and so on. The needs of the church call out to the SJ's core need for earned membership, responsibility and duty, service and caretaking. SJs get many of their own core needs met as they serve in these various capacities. Furthermore, many of the introverted SJs are content to work behind the scenes without much recognition.

The SJ will do the same thing on the home front, making sure the needs of the elderly family members are met and taking care of invalids or those who are sick. Most SJs will be steady income producers, as their primary motivating goal is to provide for the needs of their families. Stay-at-home moms who are SJs generally have hobbies that will produce some kind of income in addition to their regular duties around the house.

When taken to an extreme, a strength becomes a weakness:

➢ The SJ has difficulty receiving from others

Everyone eventually needs to be served, even the SJ who is so accustomed to doing the serving. Everyone has seasons in life when they need help from others. When this desire of the SJ to serve others is pushed to an extreme, it manifests itself in the SJ's denial that they need help, even in times when they really do. I had to come to grips with this and realize that behind this mindset is something called pride. That was a hard pill for me to swallow, but I eventually choked it down.

The other thing that showed me life was about giving and receiving was the Golden Rule, which is taken directly from Scripture:

Therefore, whatever you want others to do for you, do also the same for them – this is the Law and the Prophets (Matthew 7:12).

God didn't give the Golden Rule exclusively to people with the SJ temperament. I don't have the right to deny someone the freedom of exercising the Golden Rule in reference to me. So with this in mind, SJs should practice graciously receiving from others; after all, it's our duty.

Scriptural principle for keeping this strength in balance:

Pride comes before destruction, and an arrogant spirit before a fall (Proverbs 16:18).

☐ **STRENGTH: SJs have common sense and are always well prepared**

William D. Boyce, Ernest Thompson Seton, Daniel Carter Beard. If you recognized these names, you must be familiar with the Boy Scouts of America (BSA). These men founded the Boy Scouts in 1910. Daniel Carter Beard founded Boy Scouts Troop 1 in Flushing, New York, which is believed to be the oldest continuously chartered Boy Scout Troop in the United States. I have not profiled each of these individuals but it goes without saying there is an overwhelming SJ influence in the BSA.

The stated objectives of the BSA are referred to as *Aims of Scouting*: character development, citizenship training, and personal fitness. The BSA pursues these aims through an informal education system called the Scout method, with variations that are designed to be appropriate for the age and maturity of each membership division.

Typically, Scouts and Guides will make the three-fingered Scout Sign when reciting the promise.

On my honor, I promise that ...
 1. I will do my duty to God and the Queen.
 2. I will do my best to help others, whatever it costs me.
 3. I know the scout law, and will obey it.[4]

Why so much about the BSA? This organization is a natural for the SJ. The SJ takes to the Boy Scouts or the Girl Scouts like a duck takes to water. This is ground zero for young SJs to develop many of the natural skills they posses. Common sense and preparedness are the hallmarks of these organizations.

When I take a vacation, I think of every possible scenario that could happen, and if it is within my means to do so, I prepare for these potential events in advance. If I'm driving, I always carry in my car a first aid kit, extra water, tools, a spare tire that has air in it (which I know because I've checked it), and so on. I believe that a great symbol for the SJ would be the Swiss Army knife, the perfect emblem of preparedness with all of its tools and gadgets in one small knife. Indeed, most SJs are always prepared for just about anything.

When taken to an extreme, a strength becomes a weakness:

> ➢ The SJ worries over anticipated problems

---

[4] WOSM and WAGGGS (13 June 2001). "Report on the Discussion on the Fundamental Principles of WAGGGS and WOSM." pp. 7-8. http://www.ppoe.at/scoutdocs/relationships/wagggs_wosm_rel.pdf.

With this kind of thinking running through the SJ's mind, it's no surprise that legitimate concern can easily turn into needless worry when taken to an extreme. I have found that 99% of the things I'm concerned or worried about never come to pass. I put a lot of time and energy and sometimes money into preparing for things that never happen. I have learned to operate more like my intuitive friends who use their ingenuity to get out of a fix they haven't prepared for. Of course, even with that decision I still carry a Swiss Army knife and do preventative maintenance on my car and my home to head off any possible crises that just might occur. You never know. What can I say? –I'm an SJ.

Scriptural principle for keeping this strength in balance:

Don't worry about anything, but in everything, through prayer and petition with thanksgiving, let your requests be made known to God. And the peace of God, which surpasses every thought, will guard your hearts and your minds in Christ Jesus (Philippians 4:6-7).

A few more characteristics of the SJ–Guardian:

- Population of the SJ-Guardian in the United States: 38%

- Leadership Style: The SJ is a logistical leader, one who is great at making sure everything is there when needed.

- Time Orientation: The present; the here and now.

- Affiliates: This ties in to the SJ's core need to belong and have membership.

- Population in the organized church: The population of SJs in the church is very high; my guess is in the range of 45% to 50%. They are there because, like the Scouts, the environment is ideal for the SJ to have their core needs met. At the

In His Image

Youth With A Mission bases, the SJ will make up about 45 to 50% of the students (except in a few rare cases).

The church is blessed by the participation of the SJ population. In fact, I would go so far as to say that churches possibly would not survive without a healthy number of SJs in their congregations. If churches did manage to exist without a large percentage of SJs, it would probably be a chaotic environment. The SJ provides the glue that holds any organization together.

Chapter 12

THE NT – RATIONAL

CORE NEEDS

The third Temperament Type we will look at is the NT-Rational. If you scored **INTJ**, **INTP**, **ENTJ**, or **ENTP**, your temperament type is NT-Rational. The three primary core needs of this temperament types are as follows:

1. The need to be competent
2. The need to gain knowledge
3. The need for power and control

I call the Extraverted NTs kingdom builders and the Introverted NTs the Innovators. Out of all the temperament types, the NTs are the visionaries.

☐ CORE NEED: To be competent

Within the NT-Rational is the need to be masters at whatever grabs their interest. The core need to be competent drives them to become experts in their fields. The NT-Rational will strive to do whatever it takes to make more discoveries, come up with better theories, have more knowledge, design more unique buildings, have more money, and so on. Like the other temperament types, the core needs of the NT are inseparable: their hunger for knowledge, power, and control enhance the overall capabilities of the NT.

Source of stress in relation to this core need:

➢ Being incompetent

When NTs find themselves in situations in which they are unskilled or bored, they become very uncomfortable. If the situation is prolonged, it will become a major stressor for the NT. This is particularly true if the NT is in a job that does nothing to meet the three core needs. An example of this would be if an NT works in social services or counseling where they have to deal with the trauma that people are experiencing in their lives. The NT is much better at figuring out solutions to complex problems that relate to the physical world than they are at helping people with their emotional struggles in life. Any time emotions are part of the process, most NTs are uncomfortable. NTs rely on their intellectual ingenuity and don't give a lot of time to the development of their Feeling function, which helps any personality type interact with their emotions. This is not to say that NTs don't have a humanitarian side to them. Some of the greatest humanitarians are NTs, and one of the reasons is because many of the NTs have built financial kingdoms that have enabled them to be an active force in alleviating the suffering of their fellow human beings worldwide.

While I'm on the subject of wealth, NTs are the best at seizing opportunities to make financial gains. They are also subject to losing it all with investments that are not so sound. Many NTs will become wealthy just to lose it again, then gain it again, then lose it again, until they learn to see some of the details in the investment that make it dangerous. Not surprisingly, many of the high rollers who do their business at the New York Stock Exchange are ENTs. There will be some STPs in the mix as well.

Scriptural principle for this core need:

I raise my eyes toward the mountains. Where will my help come from? My help comes from the LORD, the Maker of heaven and earth (Psalm 121:1-2).

Reaction to the stress of feeling incompetent:

➤ They begin to obsess

When relationship issues arise with the NT, they have a more difficult time than the other temperament types at bringing a resolution to the problem. They may even avoid the person they have a conflict with, not because they are avoiding the conflict itself – NTs don't have any problems debating during a conflict – but because they don't quite know how to deal with the emotions *involved* in the conflict, whether it be their own or the other person's emotions. Linda and I have found this to be true when we are counseling married couples, and one spouse is an NT and the other is a different temperament type. Trying to get an NT to understand the personal values held by their spouse can be frustrating even for the counselor.

NTs tend to obsess over a problem until they master it. If for some reason they don't master the needed skill, they may use their time to obsess over other things.

Scriptural principle for this reaction:

Bear one another's burdens, and so fulfill the law of Christ (Galatians 6:2).

☐ CORE NEED: To gain knowledge

The NT-Rational could be compared to a large vacuum cleaner vacuuming up knowledge wherever they are. They have an insatiable thirst for knowledge. One of my family members was an NT-Rational. He would get up every morning and read the newspaper from cover to cover. Then if I happened to be there visiting him, when he was finished reading the newspaper he would begin to ask me question after question regarding current events. It was a test of my knowledge, but more than anything else, he was after the information in my head. There is no sacred ground when it comes to gaining knowledge for the NT. A great vocation for the NT is anything that has to do with research and development, since in those positions they are challenged to look at all possible ways to create what's needed or to improve upon what's there. Many NTs are inventors. They are responsible for many of the technological advancements throughout history. I believe it very likely that the following people were NTs: Louis Braille, who came up with the system of aligning raised dots on the page so that blind can read with their fingers; Jacques Cousteau, who developed the underwater camera; Robert Cailliau and Tim Berners-Lee, who developed the World Wide Web, and Bill Gates, founder of Microsoft. When it comes to connecting information, whether physical or connecting thoughts still brewing in their imaginations, none is better than the NT Rational when it comes to making technological advancements.

Scriptural principle for this core need:

> *For this reason also, since the day we heard this, we haven't stopped praying for you. We are asking that you may be filled with the knowledge of His will in all wisdom and spiritual understanding, so that you may walk worthy of the Lord, fully pleasing to Him, bearing fruit in every good work and growing in the knowledge of God (Colossians 1:9-10).*

Source of stress in relation to this core need:

> ➢ Routine and redundancy

When it comes to dealing with routine and redundant tasks, none is better than the SJ, as we've discussed previously, and none is *worse* at routine and redundancy than the NT. Once NTs have mastered something, they are ready to move on to the next challenge. To do the same thing over and over again puts them in an environment of stress or boredom, which becomes a source of stress in itself to the NT. This is why there are so few NT teachers in the lower grade levels of our educational system, which requires the teacher to educate the children through routine tasks, repetition, and redundancy. At the college level, much more creativity can be used by the professor. If they're able to teach a course that goes well beyond the fundamentals, no class session, assignment, or curriculum has to be the same for the NT professor. They will challenge students to think and figure things out for themselves. Nothing delights an NT professor more than a student who begins to make the connections and come to appropriate conclusions based on the information taught by the NT professor.

Reaction to the stress of routine and redundancy:

➢ NTs become bored and restless

You may recall that the SP is also stressed by routine and redundancy, but the NT's stress comes about because of different reasons. The SP's core needs relate to having fun and living a life filled with adventure, whereas the NT's core needs is for intellectual stimulation and ingenuity. Routine tasks don't require this kind of thinking, and thus the NT becomes bored. The NT must be challenged mentally or they will begin to leave the building, the meeting, the conference table, the church service, even if it's just going elsewhere in their minds. I used to attend conferences with an NT friend, and once he recognized the information presented by a speaker was something he had heard before, he would get up and leave. As an SJ, I would be content to take the redundant information in again because that is one of the best ways for SJ's to learn. When the session came to a close, I would have to look for my NT friend or call him on my cell phone to find him. He would usually be at a nearby bookstore or even a movie theater catching the latest Sci-Fi movie that was out.

Scriptural principle for guarding against the tendency to become bored easily reaction:

Instruct a wise man, and he will be wiser still; teach a righteous man, and he will learn more (Proverbs 9:9).

☐ CORE NEED: Power and Control

The core needs of power and control at first seem negative because we are inclined to resist those two terms for the inherent meaning that we think is behind them. With the NT-Rational, one of their primary needs is to have power and control over their own sphere of life. Having the ability to test their ideas and develop their vision without restraint is essential to the NT. This is why a good percentage of NTs, especially NTs who are extraverted, are entrepreneurs who create an environment with few restrictions. Many others may head for vocations where there are fewer restrictions and thus they will have the freedom to use their abilities the way they desire.

If you're a visionary NT, and you have become successful at the development of your vision, it will take a team to carry out that vision. In every organization, businesses or institution, someone has the vision, which is the over-arching big picture, and the companies and organizations that are continually expanding and keeping up with or leading the way with new trends and technology will have NTs somewhere in their high level team, or possibly even leading the organization itself. This doesn't mean that NTs head up all organizations, businesses and institutions, but a high percentage NTs find themselves at the forefront of progressive organizations.

When any temperament is leading, they need a team to carry out their directives. For growth and expansion to take place, power and control is needed to keep the organization headed in the right direction. Power and control can be used to everyone's benefit, or it can be used to manipulate others' lives. In this way, the right use of power is a character issue. My personal experience with NT leaders, and I have worked with and for several, is that they have the welfare of everyone in mind as they lead and grow an organization.

All temperament types, including the NT, will go through learning curves with their core needs, and over time will recognize where they need balance in their personalities so that none of their strengths are taken to an extreme and thus become weaknesses. If gaining power and control becomes the end rather than the means, more harm will be done to those whom the NT is associated with. Whenever power and control is used to accomplish a vision, its true success is measured by how much those associated with helping bring about the vision will benefit from the goal. For this to happen, NTs must filter through the principles in God's Word any decisions they make that will affect others. If the Scriptures are the foundation upon which all temperament types base their decisions, they can rest assured the decisions will be healthy for everyone concerned.

Scriptural principle for this core need:

> *This is the word of the LORD to Zerubbabel: 'Not by strength or by might, but by My Spirit,' says the LORD of Hosts (Zechariah 4:6)*

Source of stress in relation to this core need:

> ➢ Anything that restrains the NT

While it's nice to have free run of our core needs, it is rarely possible for the NT to have this freedom, since power and control must be earned. Everyone is impacted by his or her particular environment, and it takes time for those who have power to release it. That happens as trust is developed. When the environment restricts the NT from using their ingenuity and vision, it will bring about major frustration for the NT. If you're an NT and you're experiencing this frustration in your vocation, you have many options before you. Vocational changes can be tough, but if patiently planned out, you can move closer to the kind of vocation that frees you up to exercise those predisposed gifts given to you by God.

If you're in a personal relationship that you find restraining, you must learn the needed communication and conflict resolution skills to help you make progress in the relationship. No one has the right to control another individual. Some people control out of fear and some control for the purpose of personal gain. Neither is right, and both will eventually kill the relationship. Put some energy into learning some valuable communication and conflict resolution skills. You will use these skills throughout your entire life, and they will serve you well.

Reaction to imposed restraint, which makes the NT feel incompetent:

> ➤ The NT will begin to manipulate others

When the NTs are stressed through restraint, they will begin to use their intellectual ingenuity to manipulate others in order to accomplish their goals. If that doesn't work, they will eventually leave the environment or relationship. If you're an NT, good communication skills will help relieve some of the tension you feel building up and will give you clarity as to the next step you should take in an effort to experience the optimal environment for meeting your core needs, an environment where you can be at your best.

Scriptural principle for guarding against the tendency to manipulate others:

> *Do nothing out of rivalry or conceit, but in humility consider others as more important than yourselves. Everyone should look out not only for his own interests, but also for the interests of others (Philippians 2:3-4).*

☐ **STRENGTH: Intellectual ingenuity**

The intellectual ingenuity comes from the NT-Rational's hunger for knowledge combined with their intuitive capabilities of making connections with a lot of diverse information. Many NTs become inventors, software developers, lawyers, doctors, scientists, and university professors, to name a few vocations that suit this strength.

If it's a technical problem, find yourself the nearest NT-Rational, and he or she will solve it.

When taken to an extreme, a strength becomes a weakness:

> *NTs may not develop social skills*

This strength becomes a weakness when the overwhelming challenge to solve the problem overtakes the NT. If you are constantly using your ability to solve technical problems, this leaves little time for the development of social skills. This is even more pronounced in the Introverted NT. Nurturing relationships with others and attending social gatherings are secondary to testing their ingenuity, and there always seems to be a challenge before them begging to be tackled. The greater the intellectual challenge, the more the NT will work with it until they conquer it. Consider some of our great inventors such as Thomas Edison, Albert Einstein, and Jonas Salk. One thing is certain, however: the NT will eventually have to relate with people and be involved in social gatherings. For the NT-Rational, just understanding this dynamic will be helpful in sharpening those relationship skills.

Scriptural principle for keeping this strength in balance:

> *For you are called to freedom, brothers; only don't use this freedom as an opportunity for the flesh, but serve one another through love. For the entire law is fulfilled in one statement: You shall love your neighbor as yourself (Galatians 5:13-14).*

☐ **STRENGTH: NTs are visionary**

This strength usually ends up serving society well. All temperament types have vision to some degree. When I use the term vision, I am referring to seeing beyond the present to the future for what may be needed, changed or developed. The SP and SJ have vision for things that will resemble what is already here and working, perhaps with some improvements, and usually their vision is relatively short term. NFs have vision that relates to their ideals, and we will look into this in the next chapter. NTs have vision that truly recognizes what will be needed, changed, or developed in the future. No one is better at seeing trends than the NT. They make connections with information on a regular basis, a process that informs them as to the necessity or the obsolescence of things.

When taken to an extreme, a strength becomes a weakness:

> ➢ NTs continually raise the standard to the confusion of others

The ability to maintain high standards is one of those characteristics that is basically good. Not settling for the status quo and constantly improving on what has been done previously are the characteristics that keep the world an exciting, vibrant place, constantly moving forward with progress on all levels. The negative side to this trait, however, is when the NT doesn't recognize the strengths (or lack of strengths) within people of other temperament types. Most people tend to think that whatever they're good at, everyone else is as well. This is especially true of the NT. Clearly this is not the case, as often the mind of an NT is on a much higher level of reasoning. The worst scenario is when an NT parent is requiring their child of another temperament to accomplish those things the NT sees as natural. If an NT has a child who is a Feeler in the way they come to conclusions, then naturally the NT, who is a Thinker in their preference for decision-making, will have a hard time understanding why their child is just average in math. An NT (Intuitive Thinker) parent will have a difficult time understanding their child who prefers Sensing for gathering information, and therefore learns through sequential steps and is slow to catch on to the broader educational concepts that are put before him or her.

It's good to challenge your children to excel in school, but there comes a point when you need to recognize the legitimate temperament limitations of your child so that you can help him or her strengthen those areas. Otherwise, if you're constantly trying to force your "round-peg" child into a "square-peg" hole, you will slowly break down their self-confidence. This can lead to serious emotional damage that stays with them for a lifetime. This relates to the law of diminishing returns. All children will have subjects in which they excel and subjects in which they struggle. Parents need to know their children well enough to operate in the delicate balance of challenge versus encouragement. It is also the parent's responsibility to understand whether a child's struggle with a particular subject or with school in general is due to laziness or simply not being a priority (both of which can be improved with loving guidance and training), or whether it's a legitimate aspect of the child's temperament type.

Scriptural principle for keeping this strength in balance:

> *For by the grace given to me, I tell everyone among you not to think of himself more highly than he should think. Instead, think sensibly, as God has distributed a measure of faith to each one (Romans 12:3).*

☐ STRENGTH: NTs can solve complex problems

This strength is related to the NT's intellectual ingenuity. The difference is that rather than combining intuition and knowledge to come up with ideas, the NT combines intuition and thinking. This highlights their ability to figure things out on the spot through their powers of reasoning. Today, for example, you will find NTs as IT people in corporations with large computer networks. As an SJ, all I can do when the computer goes on the fritz is get frustrated. If I try to fix the problem, I usually make it worse. When NTs are faced with a similar problem, they go into action immediately, undaunted by the challenge. Furthermore, they can get extremely detailed in making the connections that will eventually solve the problem. They also seem to be very patient as they work their way through the process of locating the problem. What I see as an interruption in my production schedule the NT sees as another mental challenge and actually enjoys the process of solving a complicated problem. On a side note, unless you're an NT, don't play chess with an NT. They will checkmate you every time!

When taken to an extreme, a strength becomes a weakness:

> ➢ NTs can obsess over problem solving

Since the NT takes it as a personal challenge to solve technical problems, don't expect to see much of them until they *do* solve the problem. Another way to say it is that NTs have a tendency to obsess with the problem until it's solved. This is all right if the NT is single and has no personal life. Unfortunately, for the NT, it is rarely the case that they can be alone for hours on end immersed in the joyful challenge of unsnarling a problem. People in your life would like to have a little of your attention (and maybe more), especially if you're married. Family members may not understand why you obsess with things either. And all the while you're spending inordinate amounts of time with the problem, other commitments you've made are easy to overlook or set aside. Broken commitments never set well with those to whom you have made the commitment.

Scriptural principle for keeping this strength in balance:

> *For we don't dare classify or compare ourselves with some who commend themselves. But in measuring themselves by themselves and comparing themselves to themselves, they lack understanding. We, however, will not boast beyond measure, but according to the measure of the area of ministry that God has assigned to us (2 Corinthians 10:12-13).*

☐ **STRENGTH: NTs are direct communicators**

Normally when you are communicating with an NT, you know what's on their mind. They don't mince words or try to find a way to soften the blow if they have to deliver bad news or want to offer a differing opinion. They are interested in coming at you with their logical point of view, and it will be precisely stated when they do. In fact, if you are an NF communicating with an NT, and you approach them with your global style of communication, they will become frustrated with you and ask you to get to the point. If you're an SJ and approach the NT with your style, which is customary language, they may respond with something that makes you feel like your statement is insignificant. If you're an SP and you approach an NT with your colorful style of language, they may think it's humorous and not take you seriously. The NT has a high regard for a broad vocabulary, and you will hear them use words that you don't hear very often, and sometimes you may not even know what the word means. To the NT, a broad vocabulary reflects their intelligence level, something that appeals to the NT. Their command of language combined with their intuitive abilities makes them the great debaters they are. I think a high percentage of NTs work in our legal and political systems.

When taken to an extreme, a strength becomes a weakness:

> *Sometimes NTs seem cold and harsh to others*

The NT can wow you with their words but can unknowingly be hurtful at the same time. Because NTs are not easily hurt or offended (after all, they see everything as being open for debate), they can be insensitive in situations that require diplomacy and compassion. If their profession requires a lot of interaction with people, they will eventually learn to bring some sensitivity into appropriate situations, but in the process of learning that, they will leave some hurt feelings along the way. If they are in professions that do not require a lot of interaction with people, and they don't make a conscious effort to be more sensitive to others, it may take a lifetime for them to learn the value of this skill.

Scriptural principles for keeping this strength in balance:

Your speech should always be gracious, seasoned with salt, so that you may know how you should answer each person (Colossians 4:6).

But avoid foolish debates, genealogies, quarrels, and disputes about the law, for they are unprofitable and worthless (Titus 3:9).

☐ **STRENGTH: Ability to forecast the future**

I have mentioned this several times already, but this strength of forecasting the future is one of the characteristics of the NT that stands out and can have a great impact on organizations and society. As an SJ, I've come to appreciate this strength because it is one I don't posses. It ties in to the NT's time orientation. Both the NT and NF are future oriented in their approach to life. The NF is looking forward to that day when their personal ideal will come to fruition. The NT is constantly looking forward to future possibilities, pushing the envelope along the way. The sky and beyond is the limit.

Actually, most NTs don't see limits at all. There is always a way around, over, or through what may appear to be a limit to another personality type. The style of government in the United States is the perfect environment for the operation of this strength. NT's have the freedom to go where no one has gone before and build a kingdom as large as they desire, and they won't be penalized for doing so. This is why the United States and other countries that operate similarly to the US are progressive and expansive. If you look at the conditions of most third world countries, they are not suffering because of a lack in natural resources but a lack in forward looking, trend recognizing, creative leadership. Extraverted Intuitive Thinkers are needed at or near the top of any organization or society to provide this kind of leadership. With that said, I must also say that character development and keeping the welfare of the people in mind is a must for the NT, or the temptation for personal gain will overtake them and corruption will spoil their efforts.

I must also say that every temperament type brings with it a unique set of strengths. It takes more than just forecasting the future to accomplish lofty goals. Certain things have to be done, things that the NT temperament types are not capable of accomplishing. That successful organization, church, missionary endeavor, or society will not succeed without a mix of the required strengths of all personality types working together to accomplish the desired goal.

When taken to an extreme, a strength becomes a weakness:

> *NTs tend to miss out on the moment*

When NTs are left to themselves, their tendency is to be so future oriented that they miss out on what is happening right before their eyes. Similar but in contrast to how an SJ can be so in the moment, the NT can be so out of the moment as they stretch their minds into the future. Just as an SJ has to consciously decide to look toward the future in long-term planning (and as an SJ I have learned what it takes for me to do that), the NT can learn how to focus on the moment and not always be thinking into the future. After we put some effort into doing the things we're not naturally predisposed toward, it almost becomes second nature for us to do so. Furthermore, it's worth the effort because it enriches our life.

Scriptural principle for keeping this strength in balance:

> *Pay careful attention, then, to how you walk – not as unwise people but as wise – making the most of the time, because the days are evil (Ephesians 5:15-16).*

A few more characteristics of the NT–Rational:

- Population of the NT Rational in the United States: 12%

- Leadership Style: The NT is a *strategic leader.* They're great at seeing the big picture and devising the overall plan.

- Time Orientation: The future; they're always looking toward what's coming down the road.

- Independent: This ties into the NT's core need of power and control

- Population in the organized church: The population of NTs in the church is very low; my guess is in the range of 5% to 7%. The NTs who are in church are there because they are tapping into this new way of looking at life. The Christian perspective brings with it endless information on how to live a life designed by the creator of the universe.

I'll never forget when as a young Christian I heard Josh McDowell share his testimony about how he set out to prove the Bible wrong, and in the process ended up having the Bible prove him wrong. He committed his life to Christ. He then wrote the book *Evidence That Demands a Verdict*. Yes, it is my belief that Josh McDowell is an NT.

At the Youth With A Mission bases where Linda and I hold training sessions, NTs make up about 3% to 5% of the students except in a few rare cases.

The church is blessed by the participation of the NT population. You will find many NTs in Bible Colleges and Seminaries as Professors teaching the doctrines and theology of the Old and New Testaments.

Chapter 13

THE NF – IDEALIST

CORE NEEDS

The fourth temperament type we will look at is the NF-Idealist. If you scored **INFJ**, **INFP**, **ENFJ**, or **ENFP** you are an NF-Idealist. Your three core needs are as follows:

1. The need to be unique
2. The need to maintain integrity
3. The need to find significance and meaning in life

Out of all the temperament types, the NF relates to many of the descriptions of all of the temperaments. This is why many call the NF-Idealist the chameleon.

☐ CORE NEED: To have a unique identity

Before delving into a detailed description of the NF–Idealist, I want to reiterate how the core needs of each temperament type are knitted together and cannot be separated. This is especially true with the NF. The NF is called the Idealist because they tend to develop a picture in their mind of what their ideal is for any aspect of their life. This ideal is personal and is defined as the NF experiences life itself. Those things that impress the NF have a bearing on defining their ideal. The ideal will change with the seasons of life as different impressions make an impact on the NF-Idealist. In defining their core needs, I will also discuss the impact their ideal makes on their life and the lives of those around them.

The NF-Idealist typically lives their life as though they're on a never-ending journey in search of their identity. There will be times when they think they've made that discovery only to find out that a little further down the road, whatever they were identifying with previously is no longer compatible with their ideal of who they want to be now. On the other hand, there are certain things that become a permanent part of who they are: becoming a husband or wife; then when kids arrive, being a father or mother; then later in life, being grandfather or grandmother. You might say we all go through that, but the key difference with the NF is that each stage forms their identity and is deeply imbedded in them.

For instance, when an NF marries, they excitedly begin to take on the role of husband or wife based on their ideal for marriage. If the marriage resembles their ideal, they can and will work through areas of the relationship that don't quite fit that ideal. But if the marriage is quite different from their ideal for marriage, they will experience a lot of turmoil, especially emotionally. A big part of the turmoil is the loss of identity. They will think, *Who is this person I've become in this marriage?* Or, *Who is this person I've married?* Confusion about their identity begins to set in. Following that comes all of the emotional turmoil that is connected with the confusion.

When Linda and I do pre-marital counseling with a couple and one or both are NFs, we spend a lot of time trying to explain how their identity is tied to the ideal and how adjustments must be made to both or there will be a long, rough road ahead. In pre-marital counseling, many couples don't believe us, or if they do sincerely listen and believe we know what we're talking about, the gist of what we're saying goes right over their heads. Then, six months into their marriage, they call us for a counseling appointment because they are already struggling with how the marriage is not measuring up to the ideal of one or both NF spouses and they are confused about their identity. Of course, they don't use the same terminology I just used. They may say, *he or she is different now that we are married,* which is actually true, since most couples are on their best behavior in the dating relationship and then become who they really are after they say "I do." Or, the couple discovers they differ greatly in the way they want things done, or their goals and ambitions are vastly different, none of which was discussed thoroughly prior to marriage. All of these things tie into the NF's ideal, or how they painted the picture of marriage before they got married. This picture could have been painted even in their childhood.

One of the first things I ask an engaged couple is, what is the single most important factor in the marriage relationship? I usually get a wide variety of answers and never the one I'm looking for. My hope is the couple will recognize the value of spiritual compatibility. Several compatibility factors can make a huge impact on the marriage relationship, but in my opinion, spiritual compatibility is number one.

We have found that many NFs have already defined in their own mind their spiritual direction for life. Unfortunately, most of the time this ideal is not shared with their partner. The same is true with all of the factors that make up this magnificent portrait they've painted in their mind of who they and their spouse are going to be in the marriage. I strongly encourage any NF who is reading this to go back to Chapter Six under the sub-heading "Other Elements that Impact Our Judging Functions" and focus on the section about Expectations. The NF-Idealist's *expectations* and their *ideal* are the same. If you're an NF and you don't adjust your ideal to grow your marriage, you will kill the relationship with your expectations. This is because your expectations, or your ideal, if you will, are the same as the letter of the law in your mind. The law is written in stone and no one can live up to it. A portrait is painted on canvas and cannot be changed without completely starting over. But your portrait (ideal) is painted in your mind and *can* be changed.

As an NF-Idealist, it is important for you to remember the eternal truth of this scripture verse I majored on in chapter 6:

> *He has made us competent to be ministers of a new covenant, not of the letter, but of the Spirit; for the letter kills, but the Spirit produces life (2 Corinthians 3:6).*

This principle is clearly set forth in God's Word to show us the power of the law. We are capable of writing relationship laws. In the case of the NF temperament, this self-written law translates into their ideal. Then, their ideal will affect how they define all of their core needs. This will include their identity, whatever it is they value as being of integrity, and what is significant and meaningful to them, all of which will have very personal definitions.

Scriptural principle for this core need:

> *Now this is what the LORD says – the One who created you, Jacob, and the One who formed you, Israel – "Do not fear, for I have redeemed you; I have called you by your name; you are Mine. Everyone called by My name and created for My glory I have formed him; indeed, I have made him" (Isaiah 43:1, 7).*

Source of stress in relation to this core need:

➢ Having to conform

If an NF-Idealist has defined who they are, it will determine what they are willing to do. So when certain behavior is required of the NF, or rules are expected to be followed and pressure is applied to do so, this will cause a great deal of stress for the NF.

Raisa is like our daughter. She is an ENFP. Those four letters are almost the mirror opposite of mine. Raisa is also a gifted worship leader, and when Linda and I planted a church in Southern California, we made sure Raisa went with us. There were several things about Raisa that made her so good at leading worship. While leading worship she connects with the congregation immediately; she is unique in her style, which is very upbeat and positive; and she is very sensitive to the move of the Holy Spirit, probably more so than any worship leader I've experienced in my thirty years of ministry. From time to time, I would want her to change something about the way the worship service was going and I would talk to her about the change I wanted to make. She would usually respond with an agreeable nod of the head. Then two or three weeks would go by and I would see no change. Of course I would get frustrated. After a while, it dawned on me that I was asking Raisa to change something about who she is as the worship leader. I decided I would try a different approach. I went to Raisa and said, "Raisa, I want to bounce this idea off of you ... let me know what you think." A couple weeks went by and nothing changed, but I noticed that sometime around the third week she had implemented the change with a few little differences. Then at the end of the service she said, "What did you think of my idea to change such and such?" My response would be, "It was brilliant!" All were happy.

Asking the NF to do something that infringes upon their identity won't usually get the job done. The NF owns what they do because it is who they are. They must integrate the idea into their big picture of who they are. When they don't do what they are asked to do, it not only appears to be rebellious – some times it *is* rebellious. When we consider the rest of their core needs, it begins to make sense.

Reaction to the stress of being restrained:

> ➤ NFs simply refuse to conform

You may get a "yes I will" answer out of an NF in response to a request, but inside the NF is thinking, *It's not going to happen.*

Scriptural principle for this reaction:

> *I, therefore, the prisoner in the Lord, urge you to walk worthy of the calling you have received, with all humility and gentleness, with patience, accepting one another in love, diligently keeping the unity of the Spirit with the peace that binds us (Ephesians 4:1-3).*

☐ CORE NEED: To maintain integrity

The root of the word integrity has to do with being one or whole. In a general sense, it is related to moral virtues such as honesty and uprightness. For the NF–Idealist, there is a slight twist to the meaning of the word integrity. Once again, it ties into their ideal. Integrity to the NF is anything that lines up with *their* ideal. If the NF has had a serious encounter with Christ, they will do everything in their power to live up to the way set before them by the Spirit and the Word of God. If they have not had an encounter with Christ and the Word has no authority in their life, then integrity to the NF is simply encapsulated in their own ideal. I was once told that there is a very good chance that Adolf Hitler was a NF-Idealist. Part of his belief was that value of life could only be found in the German race. With this in mind, his integrity was not violated by the slaughtering of millions of Jews and Christians. Take abortion as another example of carrying a personal ideal to an extreme. It would be foolish to think that all temperament types except the NF-Idealist have had abortions. My point is that no matter the case, integrity for the NF is largely defined by their ideal. Don't get me wrong here. I am not saying NFs have no moral values. What I *am* saying is that the NF defines integrity by *their ideal*. How they see themselves regarding their identity, or what they see as significant and meaningful, will tie in to their concept of integrity.

Scriptural principle for this core need:

> *You supported me because of my integrity and set me in Your presence forever (Psalm 41:12).*

Source of stress in relation to this core need:

➢ Having to compromise their principles

When the ideals of the NF are violated, it feels to them like they have violated their integrity, which they have, and it breaks down the NF's self-image. They have compromised their ideal and therefore have sinned against themselves.

Reaction to the stress of having to compromise:

> ➤ The NF feels guilty and thus disassociates or goes into denial

As a result, one of two things will happen. They will begin to distance themselves from whatever they see as the negative influence or they may simply deny anything negative has taken place and will continue in the environment that is harmful to them inwardly. For example, when an NF is in an unhealthy relationship, they may go for long periods of time before they take a realistic look at what is happening to them regarding the loss of their identity and confusion about their ideal.

No other temperament type has the ability to use their imagination to the degree the NF uses theirs. In fact, when the NF experiences extended periods of stress, it is often difficult for them to distinguish between reality and fantasy. The NF can change the picture in their mind to make almost any situation livable. In some cases, it is a matter of survival for the NF. Consider the NF child who grows up in a very abusive situation. For them the fantasy world is the only safe place where they can imagine themselves as living out their ideal and thereby finding a clear identity in the process. They will detach from the negative situation and go to their favorite fantasy world. The NF who is confused about their identity and ideal needs a friend, pastor or counselor to help them find their equilibrium again, and this can take some time. The fantasy has become reality to the abused NF child.

Scriptural principles for this reaction:

> *Therefore, no condemnation now exists for those in Christ Jesus, because the Spirit's law of life in Christ Jesus has set you free from the law of sin and of death (Romans 8:1 HCSB).*

> *If we confess our sins, He is faithful and righteous to forgive us our sins and to cleanse us from all unrighteousness (1 John 1:9 HCSB).*

☐ CORE NEED: Significance and meaning in life

The NF-Idealist will give most of their time to those areas of life they see as significant and meaningful. Significance and meaning will always relate directly or indirectly to people. If they become attached to an institution it will be primarily because of the impact the institution has on the lives of people. The NF is an Intuitive Feeler, and their driving motivation is all about relationships; their own identity is developed by observing and connecting, even if it's emotionally, with someone who has impacted their life to the point where they find purpose or meaning and significance in heading in a similar direction. Throughout this process, they are putting the pieces together to come up with their ideal for life. You may be wondering if this ideal determines what the NF chooses for a career. For some NFs this is true, but in most cases, this ideal is important in their life for a season, and then they move on to something else. I've heard it said that the NF–Idealists' quest in life is to find out who they are.

Scriptural principle for this core need:

> *Then He said to them all, "If anyone wants to come with Me, he must deny himself, take up his cross daily, and follow Me. For whoever wants to save his life will lose it, but whoever loses his life because of Me will save it (Luke 9:23-24).*

Source of stress in relation to this core need:

➤ Criticism

Because of their ability to use their tremendous imagination, the NF-Idealist is a very creative temperament type. They have many ideas. Their ideas become a part of who they are, which explains why they can be sensitive to what might be said about their ideas. I'm an ESTJ, which means I live in the real world of facts, logic, and common sense, and because I'm an Extravert, whatever people hear from me is that which I have concluded. I rarely dwell in the world of imagination unless I make a decision to do so. My natural tendency is to say what I mean and mean what I say, without a lot of accompanying fluff. Because Linda and I have raised two daughters who are NFs, and also because of our close relationship with Raisa over the years, we have learned that you cannot approach the NF with the standard Sensor's approach to communication or the NT's purely intellectual appraisal of what they see in the NF's ideas. The NF can and will interpret that direct approach as criticism, not only of their idea, but criticism of them as well.

When communicating with the NF about their ideas, it's important to frame your input in a way that it doesn't come across as being critical. When I think an NF's idea won't fly because of missing elements or because it's something that has already been done, I might say to the NF, "That's very interesting! I'm curious to know how you are going to solve the issue with this or that; please keep me informed." My experience has been that the NF isn't offended or hurt by this approach and is often thankful that I pointed out something they hadn't seen. The NF has many ideas, and most of them will not come to fruition. It is helpful to them to have others give input so they don't spend a lot of time on something that even after modifications won't work well or is already in place and working effectively and therefore needs no adjusting.

Reaction to criticism:

> The NF becomes discouraged

When a person is critical about something that is meaningful and significant to the NF, they take it personally and become discouraged and perhaps even disillusioned. Keep in mind that because the NF relates so strongly to their core needs (their ideals) they take criticism personally. Instead of seeing it as constructive criticism of a suggestion, idea, or plan, they see it as belittling to them personally. If you are married to an NF, it is especially important for you to expand you communication skills and factor in this important characteristic about your NF spouse.

Scriptural principle for this reaction:

> Brothers, I do not consider myself to have taken hold of it. But one thing I do: forgetting what is behind and reaching forward to what is ahead, I pursue as my goal the prize promised by God's heavenly call in Christ Jesus (Philippians 3:13-14).

☐ **STRENGTH: NFs are skilled motivators**

When it comes to putting relationships first, the NF is at the top of the list. Their whole life is about people. Generally, you'll find the NF easy to approach, cordial, empathic, and understanding. They are very diplomatic in their relationships and realize your values are important to you. Normally they are very positive about the future and especially their ideals. They can be excellent motivators and gatherers of people as they lead the charge towards the accomplishment of their goals. They are great to have on the team and believe everyone should have input.

When taken to an extreme, a strength becomes a weakness:

➢ Others may feel manipulated by the NF

Sometimes when the NF is too focused on their ideal, it feels to those around them that they are being manipulated by the NF. If an NF is not careful, they can easily oversell their ideal, and the result will be the opposite of motivation. Their friends will scatter when they see the NF approaching. Be sensitive of others' perception of your plans and ideas, and be careful to guard against your tendency to oversell whatever it is you're involved in at the moment.

Scriptural principle for keeping this strength in balance:

> Your speech should always be gracious, seasoned with salt, so that you may know how you should answer each person (Colossians 4:6).

☐ STRENGTH: Maintains harmony in relationships

Dr. Linda Berens calls the NF the Catalyst. The definition of a catalyst is *a substance that increases the rate of a chemical reaction without itself undergoing any permanent chemical change.* When it comes to human beings, the NF is like that third element or catalyst. The change the NF brings about is not chemical but relational, bringing harmony into disparate relationships. Having an NF on the team helps the team maintain harmony. The NF will not go very long before they get into the middle of someone else's conflict, with the goal of smoothing things over and making things more harmonious for all concerned.

When taken to an extreme, a strength becomes a weakness:

> ➢ *They are uncomfortable with confrontation*

The NF likes living without strife and disharmony in their relationships. Because of that core need, they are not the best at confronting when confrontation is appropriate. They will put up with a lot of abuse in a relationship before they will confront the situation, if they do at all. One of the things I've told my NF friends for years is that conflict is not bad; it is inevitable in any relationship that has any value. If you never have conflict in a relationship, it is no more than a superficial relationship. People who have deep relationships with one another go through the good and bad and thick and thin together working things out on their journey. If you have to walk on eggshells in your relationship, I would say that either it's a one-way relationship or you're misinterpreting the person you're in relationship with. It's important to be true to yourself in a relationship and not be who you think your friend (or spouse) wants you to be. Trying to live up to their expectations of you is a losing battle. True friends accept you as you are. There will always be the need to confront. The real key, however, is to develop excellent conflict resolution skills. The better you become with these skills the easier and more successful you are with confrontation.

Scriptural principle for keeping this strength in balance:

Be angry and do not sin. Don't let the sun go down on your anger, and don't give the Devil an opportunity (Ephesians 4:26-27).

☐ **STRENGTH: NFs have very strong ideals**

I've written a lot about the NF and their ideals. The ideals for the NF are the fuel for the fire that burns within them and drives them in their life direction. If there is one motivating force in the life of the NF, it is their ideal. This is a tremendous attribute if the ideal is something that will benefit the world and not just the NF. I think of someone like Mother Teresa who gave her life to the orphans in Calcutta. Can you imagine the hardships she endured to see her ideal come to fruition? I believe Dr. Martin Luther King was also an NF who gave his life for the ideal he developed for his life's work. The NF-Idealist can be (and often are) world changers when they tap into an ideal that is God directed.

When taken to an extreme, a strength becomes a weakness:

➢ NFs believe that others should have the same ideals

When pushed to an extreme, any strength can become a weakness and in this case, even the NF's ideal can be a weakness. The NF can be so sold out to their ideal that they wonder why no one else feels as strongly about it as they do. There is nothing wrong with feeling strongly about your ideal; it becomes a problem, however, when you begin to force it upon everyone else. Not all people are going to share your feelings about what you believe in so strongly. Some may even oppose your ideal. To keep yourself from a lot of internal turmoil, you must accept this truth. Every missionary I've ever talked to believes their missions work is of utmost importance, and they wonder why everyone is not supporting their efforts. I've found that most Bible-believing Spirit-filled Christians are in fact supporting some missionary endeavor somewhere. When the dust settles, support comes as a result of relationship more than it does because of the mission itself.

Scriptural principle for keeping this strength in balance:

> *I, therefore, the prisoner in the Lord, urge you to walk worthy of the calling you have received, with all humility and gentleness, with patience, accepting one another in love, diligently keeping the unity of the Spirit with the peace that binds us (Ephesians 4:1-3).*

- ☐ **STRENGTH: NFs see the potential in people and organizations**

NFs have the ability to see the positive attributes in people as well as in organizations. The potential they see in others will always somehow tie in to or be in concert with their own ideals. This potential will also have to do with ways of making life better for individuals. When this happens, the NF has a tendency to become very involved by supporting, contributing, and promoting the lives and purposes of the people or organization(s) they support.

When taken to an extreme, a strength becomes a weakness:

> ➢ NFs can become over-involved

How many people and institutions can one person support? The NF doesn't see any limitations when it comes to their involvement in a just cause, and as a result, they often find themselves connecting with too many causes and organizations: they become over involved with all of the potential they see around them. This is especially true of the Extraverted Intuitive Feeler. We watched it happen on a regular basis with Raisa. Every once and a while, she would come over to our home and ask us to help her prioritize her life, which meant cutting out some of the conflicting priorities that seemed equally important to her. This is an area that an NF must keep under control or they will dilute their own effectiveness in their endeavors, all of which they consider to be their main direction for life.

Scriptural principle for keeping this strength in balance:

> *For which of you, wanting to build a tower, doesn't first sit down and calculate the cost to see if he has enough to complete it? Otherwise, after he has laid the foundation and cannot finish it, all the onlookers will begin to make fun of him, saying, 'This man started to build and wasn't able to finish (Luke 14:28-30).*

☐ **STRENGTH: NFs are committed counselors**

The NF-Idealist has the natural attributes of a counselor. They can be the stimulus that begins the process of healing and harmony in relationships that are struggling. They are good at seeing both sides of the story and making connections between all the issues that need to be resolved.

Many NF-Idealists choose counseling or social work as their life vocation. You will find them in the fields of psychology, social services, or ministry to name a few. Many who are in the ministry work hard to keep harmonious relationships amongst the people involved in their ministry, which is a very difficult challenge and sometimes causes frustration for the NF.

When taken to an extreme, a strength becomes a weakness:

> ➢ NFs want to rescue everyone

Having these natural counseling skills can be detrimental to the NF when they use those skills to try to fix problems in other people's lives, and they do so uninvited. When the NF detects conflict in some else's relationship, they usually have this deep urge to help them get the conflict resolved. Sometimes they tend to offer their help to someone who doesn't want it. When this happens, the NF can find him or herself on the receiving end of another person's hostility.

Scriptural principle for keeping this strength in balance:

> *A passerby who meddles in a quarrel that's not his is like one who grabs a dog by the ears (Proverbs 26:17).*

A few more characteristics of the NF–Idealist:

- Population of the NF Idealist in the United States: 12%

- Leadership Style: The NF is a diplomatic leader. The relational temperament of the NF makes them best at diplomacy.

- Time Orientation: The future; they focus on what's coming down the road.

- Affiliates: This ties in to the NF's core need of significance and meaning in life.

- Population in the organized church: The population of NFs in the church is very high; my guess is in the range of 45% to 50%. The NFs who are in church are there because the church meets so many of their core needs. The NF is the spiritual temperament type, and NFs will find themselves making connections in some spiritual environment, hopefully a Christ-centered environment. That's not always the case, however. You will find many NFs in the New Age movement, eastern religions, and about every other spiritual movement you can think of.

At the Youth With A Mission bases where Linda and I conduct training sessions, the NF will, except in a few rare cases, make up 45% to 50% of the students. This is very similar to the percentages we find in churches, especially Charismatic and Pentecostal churches. This is an extremely high percentage, especially since the NF makes up only 12% of the US population.

You will find NF's involved in prayer ministries, counseling, teaching, and any ministry where they are involved spiritually or directly with people.

Chapter 14

In Conclusion

Now that you've come to the closing chapter of the book my hope is that you have a much clearer picture of yours and others predictable behavior. Not for the purpose of "categorizing" people but for the purpose of understanding and embracing their differences. Remember the primary goal of this book is to equip people with tools that will help them minister effectively to others. I hope I've reached that goal to some degree in your life. If nothing else I hope you've become aware that all people don't see and interact with the world the same as you do. I cannot emphasize enough that the ramifications of understanding one another's approach to life based on personality and temperament characteristics is huge and then learning to appreciate the differences will change the way you live life. It will cost you some of your desires and perceptions but the overall benefit will pay tremendous dividends as you find yourself expanding your world to include all types of people and not just the types you relate well to.

I also hope that you continue to read and learn more about Type and Temperament. Consult the Bibliography in the back of the book. We just scratched the surface in this book. There is much more to learn. When you are learning about human behavior you are learning about something you are putting to work immediately, as soon as someone comes across your path. It's well worth the time invested.

In His Image

I also hope that you won't fall into the trap of psychoanalyzing everyone you come across and categorizing them with four letters or their temperament type. The quickest way to turn someone off is you telling them who they are and what they are about. It's one thing to talk to people about what you've learned about yourself but they also need the opportunity to read and make their own decision about those things they relate to when it comes to type and temperament. Yes it is important to look for indications of type in those you are close to but not for the purpose of letting them know what they are like but for the purpose of knowing how best to minister life to them. They don't need to know that you can "type" them in order for you to bless them.

One last thing. I would appreciate your input. You may e-mail me at lifecourse@me.com and I would be happy to clarify anything that you may have questions concerning.

Appendix A

The following is a short and concise outline describing four communication styles that we **ALL** use. Three of the four are inappropriate. When you develop the communication principles listed in number four you will move to a new height in your ability to communicate and resolve conflicts. This book is about developing healthy relationships so I felt it was important to leave this with you.

Four Communication Styles

1. The Aggressive Style

- It's desire is to overpower
- Is very manipulative
- It will break down a persons dignity
- Wounds deeply
- It cares only about it's own agenda
- •• *Aggressive communication is not appropriate*

2. The Passive Style

- Is a form of dishonest communication
- A passive approach never resolves conflicts
- ***Passive communication is not appropriate***

3. The Passive Aggressive Style

- Passive most of the time
- When aggression is released it can be violent
- This approach further complicates the issue
- ***The passive-aggressive style is not appropriate***

4. The Assertive Style

- **The "Assertive Style" is the appropriate way to communicate.**

A Communication Covenant:

- I will take responsibility for my feelings. i.e. *"I'm angry"*..... not ... *"you make me mad"*
- I will not allow emotions to fuel the fire while communicating. I will get my emotions under control before I start the conversation and stop the conversation if I begin to lose control of my emotions.
- I have the interest of my spouse in mind. I will do a "motives" check when stubbornness arises.

- I respect others opinions. I will listen from an "empathic" viewpoint.
- I will compromise when necessary. Appropriate communication is the key to compromise. Compromise is the key to conflict resolution.
- I will agree to disagree if necessary. Issues will come up where we are diametrically opposed. That's life. I will put it on the back burner and go back to it at a calendared time in the future.
- I will not use words for the purpose of harming my spouse. If I say something that is hurtful to my spouse, I won't defend myself, I will apologize and ask for forgiveness.

I will base my communication on the following passage:

† **Key Passage:** *Eph. 4:15 But speaking the truth in love, let us grow in every way into Him who is the head—Christ. .... 4:25 ...... Speak the truth, each one to his neighbor, because we are members of one another. 26 Be angry and do not sin. Don't let the sun go down on your anger, 27 and don't give the Devil an opportunity......... 29 No rotten talk should come from your mouth, but only what is good for the building up of someone in need, in order to give grace to those who hear.*

Bible Verse References:

Forward
Matthew 7:12
James 1:17
Matthew 6:32

Chapter 1
Psalm 139:13-16
Jeremiah 1:4-5
Genesis 4:20-22
Romans 12:3-8
Proverbs 23:7
Philippians 4:13
2 Corinthians 12:9
Acts 3:25
Genesis 2:7
1 Corinthians 9:22-23

Chapter 2
Genesis 1:26
1 Thessalonians 5:23
Romans 5:3-5
James 1:2-4
James 1:22
James 1:12-15
2 Corinthians 10:3-6
John 16:7-8

Chapter 4
Romans 12:2
Philippians 2:4
Philippians 4:13
Proverbs 26:17
2 Corinthians 5:18
Proverbs 17:17
Proverbs 10:19

Psalm 51:15
Philippians 2:3
Psalm 119:59-60
Proverbs 25:11
Deuteronomy 31:6

Chapter 5
Hebrews 11:1
Hebrews 4:12
Hebrews 11:3
1 Peter 1:13
Ephesians 4:29
Luke 14:28
Psalms 34:8
John 1:2
Luke 19:11
2 Timothy 2:14
Proverbs 1:5
Ephesians 5:15
2 Corinthians 9:8
Luke 10:40

Chapter 6
2Corinthians 3:6
1 Corinthians 12:14
1 Peter 3:7

Chapter 7
Matthew 23:23
Proverbs 29:15 and 17
Ephesians 6:1-4
Matthew 7:1-3
Colossians 3:23
Romans 12:17
1 Samuel 13:8-15
Ephesians 4:15
Philippians 4:4-8

Proverbs 16:7
Psalm 34:14
Psalm 119:15
Romans 15:13

Chapter 8
Genesis 6:22
Ephesians 5:15-16
2 Corinthians 6:4
Proverbs 14:8
James 4:6
Ecclesiastes 3:1
Ecclesiastes 3:11
Ecclesiastes 12:9
Luke 19:20
Proverbs 15:30
Proverbs 24:3-4

Chapter 9
Ephesians 4
Romans 12
1 Corinthians 12
Romans 7:5-6
Romans 7:22-25
Romans 10:8-11
John 14:6
Proverbs 27:21
Psalm 119:50
Psalm 107:20
2 Corinthians 5:17
Romans 12:1-2
John 15:1-2
Ephesians 4:21-24

Chapter 10
Galatians 5:1
Galatians 5:13

Galatians 5:22-23
Mark 16:15-18
Colossians 3:15-17
Acts 1:8
Acts 4:13
2 Timothy 2:15
Ephesians 5:15
Proverbs 4:25-27
Psalm 4:1
2 Corinthians 5:6-7

Chapter 11
1 Corinthians 12:18
Ephesians 2:19
Ephesians 4:25-27
Romans 12:14
Matthew 7:24-25
Galatians 6:9
Ephesians 6:5-8
Matthew 7:1-2
Proverbs 29:18
Proverbs 16:3
2 Corinthians 3:5-6
Matthew 7:12
Proverbs 16:18
Philippians 4:6-7

Chapter 12
Psalm 121:1-2
Galatians 6:2
Colossians 1:9-10
Proverbs 9:9
Zechariah 4:6
Philippians 2:3-4
Galatians 5:13-4
Romans 12:3
2 Corinthians 10:12-13

Colossians 4:6
Titus 3:9
Ephesians 5:15-16

Chapter 13
2 Corinthians 3:6
Isaiah 43:1,7
Ephesians 4:1-3
Psalm 41:12
Romans 8:1
1 John 1:9
Luke 9:23-24
Philippians 3:13-14
Colossians 4:6
Ephesians 4:26-27
Ephesians 4:1-3
Luke 14:28-30
Proverbs 26:17

Appendix A
Ephesians 4:15
Ephesians 4:25-29

References

Berens, Linda V. *Understanding Yourself and Others: An Introduction To Temperament 2.0. Huntington Beach Ca.:* TelosPublications, 2000

Berens, Linda V., and Dario Nardi *The 16 Personality Types: Descriptions for Self-Discovery Huntington Beach Ca.:* TelosPublications, 1999

Keirsey, David, and Marilyn Bates, *Please Understand Me.* 3rd ed. Del Mar, Calif.: Prometheus Nemesis Books, 1978.

Myers, Isabel, and Peter Myers, contributer. *Gifts Differing.* Palo Alto, Calif.: Consulting Psychologist Press, 1995.

Breinigsville, PA USA
19 February 2010
232819BV00002B/2/P